THE SOCIAL AND ECONOMIC WORKS OF JOHN RUSKIN

Printed in Great Britain by
Antony Rowe Ltd, Chippenham, Wiltshire

THE CROWN OF WILD OLIVE

John Ruskin

With a new Introduction by
Peter Cain

ROUTLEDGE / THOEMMES PRESS

Published in 1994 by
Routledge/Thoemmes Press
11 New Fetter Lane
London EC4P 4EE

The Social and Economic Works of John Ruskin
6 Volumes : ISBN 0 415 11350 4

Routledge/Thoemmes Press is a joint imprint
of Routledge and Thoemmes Antiquarian Books Ltd.

British Library Cataloguing-in-Publication Data
A CIP record of this series is available
on request from the British Library

Publisher's Note

These reprints are taken from original copies of each book. In many cases the condition of those originals is not perfect, the paper, often handmade, having suffered over time and the copy from such things as inconsistent printing pressures resulting in faint text, show-through from one side of a leaf to the other, the filling in of some characters, and the break up of type. The publisher has gone to great lengths to ensure the quality of these reprints but points out that certain characteristics of the original copies will, of necessity, be apparent in reprints thereof.

INTRODUCTION

The Crown of Wild Olive is a book written in a different style to Ruskin's earlier, and better known, socio-economic writings, *Unto This Last* and *Munera Pulveris*. The latter were written as essays in the heavyweight journals of the day and they represented Ruskin's attempt to challenge conventional political economy, and the business ethics derived from them, by subjecting the assumptions upon which they were based to close scrutiny. Despite the brilliance of Ruskin's writing, to be fully appreciated both books, and more especially *Munera Pulveris*, need the same careful and attentive reading as any formal economics text.

By contrast, the four main parts of *The Crown of Wild Olive* were given as lectures which, as Ruskin said, 'though delivered at considerable intervals of time, and in different places, were not prepared without reference to each other' (para. 9). The lecture 'Work' was given to a working men's organization in 1865 and that entitled 'War' was delivered to young soldiers in Woolwich in the same year. 'Traffic', on the other hand, was given before an audience of Bradford businessmen in the year previous. Carefully revised versions of these three lectures, together with the introduction, were first published in 1866 under the present title. The book sold well; and when a fourth edition was called for in 1873, a further lecture on 'The Future of England', given in 1869, was added and also the curious appendix where Ruskin summarized parts of his friend Carlyle's monumental study *Frederick the Great.* Despite revisions of the original text, the lecture format meant that the Ruskinian message was conveyed more simply and directly than in the earlier works. Faced with the need to pass the essentials of his thought to a great variety of audiences who could not be assumed to know much about them beforehand, Ruskin employed a very effective rhetorical style which makes *The Crown of Wild Olive* an excellent introduction to many of his leading ideas.

One of Ruskin's principal claims in his earlier works had been that wealth was an intrinsic quality in things, embodied either in commodities created by man or existing naturally. The main purpose of social existence – and of a high position in life which gave command over resources and labour – was to produce as many people as possible capable of appreciating this wealth. However, a business ethic driven by the selfish individualism described by classical economics, and encouraging an unchecked lust for profit, could achieve its aims simply by trading on the ignorance and folly of mankind, but would create a world of poverty and 'illth' in the process.

In the introduction to *The Crown of Wild Olive*, Ruskin offered a concrete example of this phenomenon and one with a startlingly modern ring to it (paras. 1–8). He evoked the beauty of the rivers and streams of a part of Surrey he knew well and condemned in vivid detail, 'the insolent defiling of these springs by the human herds that drink of them' and the 'festering scum' and 'black slime' left on the waters which no-one cared to remove.

He then shifted his readers' attention to a set of ugly iron railings placed around a public house in Croyden which had cost far more than cleaning the river would have done and which served no useful purpose.

> Now how does it come to pass that this work was done instead of the other: that the strength and the life of the English operative was spent in defiling ground, instead of redeeming it, and in producing an entirely (in that place) valueless, piece of metal, which can neither be eaten nor breathed, instead of medicinal fresh air and pure water?

The answer, of course, was that there was no profit to be gained from cleaning rivers and therefore a part of the natural wealth of Britain was extinguished: but there was plenty to be gained from persuading Croyden publicans to buy iron railings 'to make themselves more conspicuous to drunkards'. And thus, for foolish reasons, men were put to work making iron in dangerous conditions (dangers which Ruskin underlined by reprinting a newspaper account of a horrific accident in a foundry). By inciting ignorant people to indulge their follies, capitalists robbed society as effectively as had the barons of old, only 'one comes as an open robber, the other as a cheating pedlar'. But the plunder was not obvious; indeed, unlike his predatory predecessors, the seller of useless iron is 'thanked as a public benefactor, and promoter of commercial prosperity'.

Having offered this riveting contrast, Ruskin could then enforce the wider conclusion that 'the real good of all work, and of all commerce, depends on the final intrinsic worth of the thing you make, or get by it'. Unfortunately, the public, supported by orthodox economists, continued to believe that 'business is always good, whether it be busy in mischief or benefit; and that buying and selling are always salutary, whatever the intrinsic worth of what you buy or sell'. It would be difficult to find a more pertinent, or better written, illustration of Ruskin's central principle that 'there is no wealth but life' (*Unto This Last*, para. 77) in any other of his works.

The essays in *The Crown of Wild Olive* are particularly useful in bringing into focus Ruskin's Carlylean concern with the question of social leadership and the need for a revitalized aristocracy. (Even the odd appendix, with its commentary on selected passages from Carlyle's biography of Frederick the Great, fitted into this overall theme, since Ruskin thought Frederick an exemplary leader of men, from whose life much could be learned.) Ruskin derived his idea of nobility directly from Plato – at one point he quotes extensively from the Platonic dialogue *Critias* – and his warm feeling for More's *Utopia* undoubtedly came from the fact that both acknowledged Plato as their master. As in Plato, the role of the aristocracy was to govern wisely and to do this effectively it had to avoid the corrupting force of personal wealth which lured men away from the pursuit of their public duties:

> riches – so far from being necessary to noblesse – are adverse to it. So utterly adverse, that the first character of the Nobilities which have founded great dynasties in the world is to be poor: – often poor by oath – always poor by generosity (para. 133).

A true aristocracy would have no difficulty in exerting its authority over the masses. A world in which the masters did no work but engrossed all the wealth was ripe for anarchy and, now, 'by general misgovernment,...we have created in Europe a vast populace ...which has lost even the power and conception of reverence' (para. 137).

Ruskin linked this to the main themes of his earlier social criticism in the claim that 'all our hearts have been betrayed by the plausible impiety of the modern economist telling us that "To do the best for ourselves is finally to do the best for others"' (para. 82). Wealth ill-gotten through capitalist rapacity could only bring social disaster eventually: 'whenever money is the principal object of life with either man or nation, it is both got ill and spent ill; and does harm both in the getting and the spending' (para. 34). In his lecture 'Traffic', he applied this kind of thinking to the art and architecture of Britain. Only societies with noble aims could produce great art and Britain was devoted to 'getting on' rather than to virtue, and had made the 'forbidden deity', Mammon, her inspiration:

> But if you can fix some conception of a true human state of life to be striven for – life good for all men, as for yourselves...then, in so sanctifying wealth into 'commonwealth', all your art, your literature, your daily labours, your domestic affection, and citizen's duty, will join and increase into one magnificent harmony.

Ruskin , of course, is famous for his attacks on mechanization although his hostility to it has been exaggerated and the link between his views on machinery and his arguments about leadership has often been missed. What worried Ruskin about the wholesale application of machines was that he believed them to be responsible for further concentrating income and wealth in the hands of the relatively few great owners of property with the inevitable effect of increasing poverty and the threat of anarchy, and stimulating the demand for the luxury which had such a corrupting effect on society's natural leaders (paras 153–7).

The third lecture in this collection, 'War' may, at first sight, seem rather remote from the matter discussed above, but it illustrates some important themes in Ruskin's work and highlights some of the limitations of his social philosophy. Ruskin had a strong sympathy with the heroic, chivalric ideal of warfare. He went so far as to claim that

> no great art ever yet rose on earth, but among a nation of soldiers. There is no art among a shepherd people if it remain at peace. There is no art among an agricultural people if it remain at peace. Commerce is barely consistent with fine art; but cannot produce it. Manufacture not only is unable to produce it, but invariably destroys whatever seeds of it exist.
>
> (para. 86)

Having said this, Ruskin was quick to recognize the numerous ignoble ends which warfare could serve. But there was an even more fundamental flaw in his reasoning. Ruskin recognized that modern industry and commerce were more or less incompatible with chivalric war. Mechanized warfare made a mockery of the idea of personal heroism on which the chivalric concept was based and was horrifically destructive not only of property but of people. And did not Ruskin also say that success in leadership depended on 'multiplying good men' and on having 'the greatest possible number of good and brave Englishmen'? (para. 145).

The only way in which Ruskin could rescue the chivalric concept was by suggesting a return to a pre-capitalist society. He pinned his hopes for the future upon converting capitalist industrialists from the predatory pursuit of profit to a life based on service to the community taking his model from the ancient Greek polis and the medieval guild system. In this world mechanization would be tamed and the hero could live again. This was, of course an impossibly Utopian demand though Ruskin refused to recognize it as such. His difficulties here were a sign of the fact that, despite the profundity of his critique of capitalist civilization, Ruskin was incapable of offering a plausible alternative to it. The fact that Ruskin provided the emergent British labour movement with some of its most profound weapons of attack against capitalism should not obscure the fact that Ruskin's own preferred society lay in the mythical past rather than the possible future.

Peter Cain,
University of Birmingham,
1994

BIBLIOGRAPHICAL NOTE

All serious scholarly studies of Ruskin must refer to *The Works of John Ruskin*, edited by E. T. Cook and A. Wedderburn in 39 volumes between 1903 and 1912. Despite its many faults, this edition is still indispensable: for example, vol. XVII contains a great deal of material in correspondence, letters to the press etc., on economic matters which make a valuable supplement to the material in this series. The best general introduction to Ruskin as a thinker is G. P. Landow, *Ruskin* (1985), in the Oxford University Press Past Masters series. To understand Ruskin's place in the evolving scheme of British criticism of capitalist civilization, Raymond Williams, *Culture and Society, 1780–1850* (1958) is still very useful but it should be supplemented with J. F. Spear, *Dreams of an English Eden: Ruskin and his Tradition in Social Criticism* (1984) which links Ruskin backwards to Carlyle and forwards to Morris. On Ruskin's economic ideas, J. A. Hobson's *John Ruskin, Social Reformer* (1898) still has considerable value and is reprinted in this series. In modern times, the economic writings have been effectively analyzed in an essay by A. J. Lee in R. Hewison (ed.), *New Approaches to Ruskin* (1979), a collection of general interest. More substantial critiques of Ruskin's ideas can be found in J. T. Fain, *Ruskin and the Economists* (1956); J. A. Sherburne, *John Ruskin and the Ambiguities of Abundance* (1972), which is rich not only in analysis but in its comparisons of Ruskin's ideas with those of other critics of orthodoxy; Noel Thompson, *The Market and its Critics: Socialist Political Economy in Nineteenth Century Britain* (1988) which has a chapter on Ruskin: and P. D. Antony, *John Ruskin's Labour. A Study in Ruskin's Social Theory*, perhaps the most readable critique and the best at linking Ruskin's post-1860 writings with his earlier work. The hostile reception of Ruskin's economic writings is registered in J. L. Bradley (ed.), *Ruskin: The Critical Heritage* (1984).

THE

CROWN OF WILD OLIVE.

FOUR LECTURES

ON

INDUSTRY AND WAR.

BY

JOHN RUSKIN, M.A.

HONORARY STUDENT OF CHRISTCHURCH, AND SLADE PROFESSOR OF FINE ART.

'And indeed it should have been of gold, had not Jupiter been so poor.'
ARISTOPHANES (*Plutus*).

LONDON:
SMITH, ELDER, & CO., 15 WATERLOO PLACE.
G. ALLEN, HEATHFIELD COTTAGE, KESTON, KENT.
1873.

CONTENTS.

PAGE

INTRODUCTORY 1

LECTURE I.

WORK 21

LECTURE II.

TRAFFIC 62

LECTURE III.

WAR 98

LECTURE IV.

THE FUTURE OF ENGLAND 146

APPENDIX.

NOTES ON THE ECONOMIES OF THE KINGS OF PRUSSIA 177

THE

CROWN OF WILD OLIVE.

INTRODUCTION.*

1. TWENTY YEARS ago, there was no lovelier piece of lowland scenery in South England, nor any more pathetic, in the world, by its expression of sweet human character and life, than that immediately bordering on the sources of the Wandle, and including the low moors of Addington, and the villages of Beddington and Carshalton, with all their pools and streams. No clearer or diviner waters ever sang with constant lips of the hand which 'giveth rain

* Called the 'Preface' in former editions; it is one of my bad habits to put half my books into preface. Of this one, the only prefatory thing I have to say is that most of the contents are stated more fully in my other volumes; but here, are put in what, at least, I meant to be a more popular form, all but this introduction, which was written very carefully to be read, not spoken, and the last lecture on the Future of England, with which, and the following notes on it, I have taken extreme pains.

from heaven;' no pastures ever lightened in spring-time with more passionate blossoming; no sweeter homes ever hallowed the heart of the passer-by with their pride of peaceful gladness,—fain-hidden—yet full-confessed. The place remains (1870) nearly unchanged in its larger features; but, with deliberate mind I say, that I have never seen anything so ghastly in its inner tragic meaning,—not in Pisan Maremma,—not by Campagna tomb,—not by the sand-isles of the Torcellan shore,—as the slow stealing of aspects of reckless, indolent, animal neglect, over the delicate sweetness of that English scene: nor is any blasphemy or impiety, any frantic saying, or godless thought, more appalling to me, using the best power of judgment I have to discern its sense and scope, than the insolent defiling of those springs by the human herds that drink of them. Just where the welling of stainless water, trembling and pure, like a body of light, enters the pool of Carshalton, cutting itself a radiant channel down to the gravel, through warp of feathery weeds, all waving, which it traverses with its deep threads of clearness, like the chalcedony in moss-agate, starred here and there with the white grenouillette; just in the very rush and murmur of the first spreading currents, the human wretches of the place cast their street and house foulness; heaps of dust and slime, and broken shreds of old metal, and rags of putrid clothes; which, having neither energy to cart away, nor decency enough to dig into the ground, they thus shed into the stream, to diffuse what venom of it will float and melt, far away, in all places where God meant those waters to bring joy and health. And, in a little pool behind some houses farther in the village, where another spring rises, the shattered stones of the well, and of the little fretted channel which was long ago built and traced for it by gentler hands, lie scattered, each from each, under a ragged bank of mortar, and scoria, and bricklayer's refuse, on one side, which the clean water nevertheless chastises to purity; but it cannot conquer the dead earth beyond: and there, circled and coiled under festering scum, the stagnant edge of the pool effaces itself into a slope of black slime, the accumulation of indolent years. Half-a-dozen men, with one day's work, could cleanse those pools, and trim the flowers about their banks, and make every breath of summer air above them rich with cool balm; and every glittering wave medicinal, as if it ran, troubled only of angels, from the porch of Bethesda. But that day's work is never given, nor, I suppose, will be; nor will any joy be possible to heart of man, for evermore, about those wells of English waters.

2. When I last left them, I walked up slowly

through the back streets of Croydon, from the old church to the hospital; and, just on the left, before coming up to the crossing of the High Street, there was a new public-house built. And the front of it was built in so wise manner, that a recess of two feet was left below its front windows, between them and the street-pavement; a recess too narrow for any possible use, (for even if it had been occupied by a seat, as in old time it might have been, everybody walking along the street would have fallen over the legs of the reposing wayfarer). But, by way of making this two feet depth of freehold land more expressive of the dignity of an establishment for the sale of spirituous liquors, it was fenced from the pavement by an imposing iron railing, having four or five spear-heads to the yard of it, and six feet high; containing as much iron and iron-work, indeed, as could well be put into the space; and by this stately arrangement, the little piece of dead ground within, between wall and street, became a protective receptacle of refuse; cigar ends, and oyster-shells, and the like, such as an open-handed English street-populace habitually scatters; and was thus left, unsweepable by any ordinary methods. Now the iron bars which, uselessly (or in great degree worse than uselessly) enclosed this bit of ground, and made it pestilent, represented a quantity of work which would have cleansed the Carshalton pools three times over; of work, partly cramped and perilous, in the mine; partly grievous and horrible, at the furnace: partly foolish and sedentary, of ill-taught students making bad designs: work from the beginning to the last fruits of it, and in all the branches of it, venomous, deathful,* and miserable.

3. Now, how did it come to pass that this work was done instead of the other; that the strength and life of the English operative were spent in defiling ground, instead of redeeming it; and in producing an entirely (in that place) valueless, piece of metal, which can neither be eaten nor breathed, instead of medicinal fresh air and pure water?

4. There is but one reason for it, and at present a conclusive one,—that the capitalist can charge

* 'A fearful occurrence took place a few days since, near Wolverhampton. Thomas Snape, aged nineteen, was on duty as the "keeper" of a blast furnace at Deepfield, assisted by John Gardner, aged eighteen, and Joseph Swift, aged thirty-seven. The furnace contained four tons of molten iron, and an equal amount of cinders, and ought to have been run out at 7.30 P.M. But Snape and his mates, engaged in talking and drinking, neglected their duty, and, in the meantime, the iron rose in the furnace until it reached a pipe wherein water was contained. Just as the men had stripped, and were proceeding to tap the furnace, the water in the pipe, converted into steam, burst down its front and let loose on them the molten metal, which instantaneously consumed Gardner; Snape, terribly burnt, and mad with pain, leaped into the canal and then ran home and fell dead on the threshold; Swift survived to reach the hospital, where he died too.'

per-centage on the work in the one case, and cannot in the other. If, having certain funds for supporting labour at my disposal, I pay men merely to keep my ground in order, my money is, in that function, spent once for all; but if I pay them to dig iron out of my ground, and work it, and sell it, I can charge rent for the ground, and per-centage both on the manufacture and the sale, and make my capital profitable in these three bye-ways. The greater part of the profitable investment of capital, in the present day, is in operations of this kind, in which the public is persuaded to buy something of no use to it, on production or sale of which the capitalist may charge per-centage; the said public remaining all the while under the persuasion that the per-centages thus obtained are real national gains, whereas, they are merely filchings out of light pockets, to swell heavy ones.

5. Thus, the Croydon publican buys the iron railing, to make himself more conspicuous to drunkards. The public-housekeeper on the other side of the way presently buys another railing, to out-rail him with. Both are, as to their *relative* attractiveness, just where they were before; but they have both lost the price of the railings; which they must either themselves finally lose, or make their aforesaid customers, the amateurs of railings, pay,

by raising the price of their beer, or adulterating it. Either the publicans, or their customers, are thus poorer by *precisely what the capitalist has gained;* and the value of the industry itself, meantime, has been lost to the nation; the iron bars, in that form and place being wholly useless.

6. It is this mode of taxation of the poor by the rich which is referred to in the text (§ 34), in comparing the modern acquisitive power of capital with that of the lance and sword; the only difference being that the levy of black mail in old times was by force, and is now by cozening. The old rider and reiver frankly quartered himself on the publican for the night;—the modern one merely makes his lance into an iron spike, and persuades his host to buy it. One comes as an open robber, the other as a cheating pedler; but the result, to the injured person's pocket, is absolutely the same. Of course many useful industries mingle with, and disguise the useless ones; and in the habits of energy aroused by the struggle, there is a certain direct good. It is better to spend four thousand pounds in making a gun, and then to blow it to pieces, than to pass life in idleness. Only do not let the proceeding be called 'political economy.'

7. There is also a confused notion in the minds of many persons, that the gathering of the property

of the poor into the hands of the rich does no ultimate harm; since, in whosesoever hands it may be, it must be spent at last; and thus, they think, return to the poor again. This fallacy has been again and again exposed; but, granting the plea true, the same apology may, of course, be made for black mail, or any other form of robbery. It might be (though practically it never is) as advantageous for the nation that the robber should have the spending of the money he extorts, as that the person robbed should have spent it. But this is no excuse for the theft. If I were to put a turnpike on the road where it passes my own gate, and endeavour to exact a shilling from every passenger, the public would soon do away with my gate, without listening to any plea on my part that 'it was as advantageous to them, in the end, that I should spend their shillings, as that they themselves should.' But if, instead of out-facing them with a turnpike, I can only persuade them to come in and buy stones, or old iron, or any other useless thing, out of my ground, I may rob them to the same extent, and be, moreover, thanked as a public benefactor, and promoter of commercial prosperity. And this main question for the poor of England—for the poor of all countries—is wholly omitted in every common treatise on the subject of wealth. Even by the labourers themselves, the operation of capital is regarded only in its effect on their immediate interests; never in the far more terrific power of its appointment of the kind and the object of labour. It matters little, ultimately, how much a labourer is paid for making anything; but it matters fearfully what the thing is, which he is compelled to make. If his labour is so ordered as to produce food, and fresh air, and fresh water, no matter that his wages are low;—the food and fresh air and water will be at last there; and he will at last get them. But if he is paid to *destroy* food and fresh air, or to produce iron bars instead of them,—the food and air will finally *not* be there, and he will *not* get them, to his great and final inconvenience.

8. I have been long accustomed, as all men engaged in work of investigation must be, to hear my statements laughed at for years, before they are examined or believed; and I am generally content to wait the public's time. But it has not been without displeased surprise that I have found myself totally unable, as yet, by any repetition, or illustration, to force this plain thought into my readers' heads,—that the wealth of nations, as of men, consists in substance, not in ciphers; and that the real good of all work, and of all commerce, depends on the final intrinsic worth of the thing you make, or get by

it.* This is a 'practical' enough statement, one would think: but the English public has been so possessed by its modern school of economists with the notion that Business is always good, whether it be busy in mischief or in benefit; and that buying and selling are always salutary, whatever the intrinsic worth of what you buy or sell, that it seems impossible to gain so much as a patient hearing for any inquiry respecting the substantial result of our eager modern labour.

9. I have never felt more checked by the sense of this impossibility than in arranging the heads of the following lectures, which, though delivered at considerable intervals of time, and in different places, were not prepared without reference to each other. Their connection would, however, have been made far more distinct, if I had not been prevented, by what I feel to be another great difficulty in addressing English audiences, from enforcing, with any decision, the common, and to me the most important, part of their subjects. I chiefly desired to question my hearers—operatives, merchants, and soldiers, as to the ultimate meaning of the *business* they had in hand; and to know from them what they expected or intended their manufacture to come to, their selling to come to, and their killing to come

* Compare Preface to *Munera Pulveris*.

to. That appeared the first point needing determination before I could speak to them with any real utility or effect. 'You craftsmen—salesmen—swordsmen,—do but tell me clearly what you want; then, if I can say anything to help you, I will; and if not, I will account to you as I best may for my inability.'

10. But in order to put this question into any terms, one had first of all to face a difficulty—to me for the present insuperable,—the difficulty of knowing whether to address one's audience as believing, or not believing, in any other world than this. For if you address any average modern English company as believing in an Eternal life; and then endeavour to draw any conclusions from this assumed belief, as to their present business, they will forthwith tell you that 'what you say is very beautiful, but it is not practical.' If, on the contrary, you frankly address them as *un*believers in Eternal life, and try to draw any consequences from that unbelief,—they immediately hold you for an accursed person, and shake off the dust from their feet at you.

11. And the more I thought over what I had got to say, the less I found I could say it, without some reference to this intangible or intractable question. It made all the difference, in asserting any principle of war, whether one assumed that a discharge of artillery would merely knead down a certain

quantity of once living clay into a level line, as in a brick-field; or whether, out of every separately Christian-named portion of the ruinous heap, there went out, into the smoke and dead-fallen air of battle, some astonished condition of soul, unwillingly released. It made all the difference, in speaking of the possible range of commerce, whether one assumed that all bargains related only to visible property—or whether property, for the present invisible, but nevertheless real, was elsewhere purchasable on other terms. It made all the difference, in addressing a body of men subject to considerable hardship, and having to find some way out of it—whether one could confidently say to them, 'My friends,—you have only to die, and all will be right;' or whether one had any secret misgiving that such advice was more blessed to him that gave than to him that took it.

12. And therefore the deliberate reader will find, throughout these lectures, a hesitation in driving points home, and a pausing short of conclusions which he will feel I would fain have come to;—hesitation which arises wholly from this uncertainty of my hearers' temper. For I do not speak, nor have I ever spoken, since the time of first forward youth, in any proselytizing temper, as desiring to persuade any one to believe anything; but, whomsoever I

venture to address, I take, for the time, his creed as I find it; and endeavour to push it into such vital fruit as it seems capable of. Thus, it is a creed with a great part of the existing English people, that they are in possession of a book which tells them, straight from the lips of God, all they ought to do, and need to know. I have read that book, with as much care as most of them, for some forty years; and am thankful that, on those who trust it, I can press its pleadings. My endeavour has been uniformly to make them trust it more deeply than they do; trust it, not in their own favourite verses only, but in the sum of all; trust it, not as a fetish or talisman, which they are to be saved by daily repetitions of; but as a Captain's order, to be heard and obeyed at their peril. I was always encouraged by supposing my hearers to hold such belief. To these, if to any, I once had hope of addressing, with acceptance, words which insisted on the guilt of pride, and the futility of avarice; from these, if from any, I once expected ratification of a political economy, which asserted that the life was more than the meat, and the body than raiment; and these, it once seemed to me, I might ask, without being accused of fanaticism, not merely in doctrine of the lips, but in the bestowal of their heart's treasure, to separate themselves from the crowd of whom it is written, 'After all these things do the Gentiles seek.'

13. It cannot, however, be assumed, with any semblance of reason, that a general audience is now wholly, or even in majority, composed of these religious persons. A large portion must always consist of men who admit no such creed; or who, at least, are inaccessible to appeals founded on it. And as, with the so-called Christian, I desired to plead for honest declaration and fulfilment of his belief in life,—with the so-called Infidel, I desired to plead for an honest declaration and fulfilment of his belief in death. The dilemma is inevitable. Men must either hereafter live, or hereafter die; fate may be bravely met, and conduct wisely ordered, on either expectation; but never in hesitation between ungrasped hope, and unconfronted fear. We usually believe in immortality, so far as to avoid preparation for death; and in mortality, so far as to avoid preparation for anything after death. Whereas, a wise man will at least hold himself ready for one or other of two events, of which one or other is inevitable; and will have all things ended in order, for his sleep, or left in order, for his awakening.

14. Nor have we any right to call it an ignoble judgment, if he determine to end them in order, as for sleep. A brave belief in life is indeed an

enviable state of mind, but, as far as I can discern, an unusual one. I know few Christians so convinced of the splendour of the rooms in their Father's house, as to be happier when their friends are called to those mansions, than they would have been if the Queen had sent for them to live at Court: nor has the Church's most ardent 'desire to depart, and be with Christ,' ever cured it of the singular habit of putting on mourning for every person summoned to such departure. On the contrary, a brave belief in death has been assuredly held by many not ignoble persons; and it is a sign of the last depravity in the Church itself, when it assumes that such a belief is inconsistent with either purity of character, or energy of hand. The shortness of life is not, to any rational person, a conclusive reason for wasting the space of it which may be granted him; nor does the anticipation of death, to-morrow, suggest, to any one but a drunkard, the expediency of drunkenness to-day. To teach that there is no device in the grave, may indeed make the deviceless person more contented in his dullness; but it will make the deviser only more earnest in devising: nor is human conduct likely, in every case, to be purer, under the conviction that all its evil may in a moment be pardoned, and all its wrong-doing in a moment redeemed; and that the sigh of repentance, which purges the guilt of the past, will waft the soul into a felicity which forgets its pain,—than it may be under the sterner, and to many not unwise minds, more probable, apprehension, that 'what a man soweth that shall he also reap'—or others reap,—when he, the living seed of pestilence, walketh no more in darkness, but lies down therein.

15. But to men for whom feebleness of sight, or bitterness of soul, or the offence given by the conduct of those who claim higher hope, may have rendered this painful creed the only possible one, there is an appeal to be made, more secure than any which can be addressed to happier persons. Might not a preacher, in comfortless, but faithful, zeal—from the poor height of a grave-hillock for his Hill of Mars, and with the Cave of the Eumenides at his side,—say to them thus: Hear me, you dying men, who will soon be deaf for ever. For these others, at your right hand and your left, who look forward to a state of infinite existence, in which all their errors will be overruled, and all their faults forgiven;—for these, who, stained and blackened in the battle smoke of mortality, have but to dip themselves for an instant in the font of death, and to rise renewed of plumage, as a dove that is covered with silver, and her feathers like gold;—for these, indeed, it may

be permissible to waste their numbered moments, through faith in a future of innumerable hours; to these, in their weakness, it may be conceded that they should tamper with sin which can only bring forth fruit of righteousness, and profit by the iniquity which, one day, will be remembered no more. In them, it may be no sign of hardness of heart to neglect the poor, over whom they know their Master is watching; and to leave those to perish temporarily, who cannot perish eternally. But, for *you* there is no such hope, and therefore no such excuse. This fate, which you ordain for the wretched, you believe to be all their inheritance; you may crush them, before the moth, and they will never rise to rebuke you;—their breath, which fails for lack of food, once expiring, will never be recalled to whisper against you a word of accusing;—they and you, as you think, shall lie down together in the dust, and the worms cover you;—and for them there shall be no consolation, and on you no vengeance,—only the question murmured above your grave: 'Who shall repay him what he hath done?' Is it therefore easier for you, in your heart, to inflict the sorrow for which there is no remedy? Will you take, wantonly, this little all of his life from your poor brother, and make his brief hours long to him with pain? Will you be more prompt to the injustice which can never be

2

redressed; and more niggardly of the mercy which you *can* bestow but once, and which, refusing, you refuse for ever?

16. I think better of you, even of the most selfish, than that you would act thus, well understanding your act. And for yourselves, it seems to me, the question becomes not less grave when brought into these curt limits. If your life were but a fever fit,—the madness of a night, whose follies were all to be forgotten in the dawn, it might matter little how you fretted away the sickly hours,—what toys you snatched at or let fall,—what visions you followed, wistfully, with the deceived eyes of sleepless phrenzy. Is the earth only an hospital? are health and heaven to come? *Then* play, if you care to play, on the floor of the hospital dens. Knit its straw into what crowns please you; gather the dust of it for treasure, and die rich in that, though clutching at the black motes in the air with your dying hands;—and yet, it may be well with you. But if this life be *no* dream, and the world no hospital, but your palace-inheritance;—if all the peace and power and joy you can ever win, must be won now, and all fruit of victory gathered here, or never;—will you still, throughout the puny totality of your life, weary yourselves in the fire for vanity? If there is no rest which remaineth for you,

is there none you might presently take? was this grass of the earth made green for your shroud only, not for your bed? and can you never lie down *upon* it, but only *under* it? The heathen, in their saddest hours, thought not so. They knew that life brought its contest, but they expected from it also the crown of all contest: No proud one! no jewelled circlet flaming through Heaven above the height of the unmerited throne; only some few leaves of wild olive, cool to the tired brow, through a few years of peace. It should have been of gold, they thought; but Jupiter was poor; this was the best the god could give them. Seeking a better than this, they had known it a mockery. Not in war, not in wealth, not in tyranny, was there any happiness to be found for them—only in kindly peace, fruitful and free. The wreath was to be of *wild* olive, mark you:—the tree that grows carelessly, tufting the rocks with no vivid bloom, no verdure of branch; only with soft snow of blossom, and scarcely fulfilled fruit, mixed with grey leaf and thorn-set stem; no fastening of diadem for you but with such sharp embroidery! But this, such as it is, you may win, while yet you live; type of grey honour, and sweet rest.* Free-heartedness, and graciousness, and undisturbed trust, and requited love, and the sight of the peace of others, and the

* μελιτόεσσα, ἀέθλων γ' ἕνεκεν.

ministry to their pain ; these, and the blue sky above you, and the sweet waters and flowers of the earth beneath ; and mysteries and presences, innumerable, of living things, — may yet be here your riches ; untormenting and divine : serviceable for the life that now is ; nor, it may be, without promise of that which is to come.

LECTURE I.

WORK.

Delivered before the Working Men's Institute, at Camberwell.

17. MY FRIENDS,—I have not come among you to-night to endeavour to give you an entertaining lecture; but to tell you a few plain facts, and ask you a few plain questions. I have seen and known too much of the struggle for life among our labouring population, to feel at ease, under any circumstances, in inviting them to dwell on the trivialities of my own studies; but, much more, as I meet to-night, for the first time, the members of a working Institute established in the district in which I have passed the greater part of my life, I am desirous that we should at once understand each other, on graver matters. I would fain tell you, with what feelings, and with what hope, I regard this Institute, as one of many such, now happily established throughout England, as well as in other

countries; and preparing the way for a great change in all the circumstances of industrial life; but of which the success must wholly depend upon our clearly understanding the conditions, and above all, the necessary *limits* of this change. No teacher can truly promote the cause of education, until he knows the mode of life for which that education is to prepare his pupil. And the fact that he is called upon to address you, nominally, as a 'Working Class,' must compel him, if he is in any wise earnest or thoughtful, to enquire in the outset, on what you yourselves suppose this class-distinction has been founded in the past, and must be founded in the future. The manner of the amusement, and the matter of the teaching, which any of us can offer you, must depend wholly on our first understanding from you, whether you think the distinction heretofore drawn between working men and others, is truly or falsely founded. Do you accept it as it stands? do you wish it to be modified? or do you think the object of education is to efface it, and enable us to forget it for ever?

18. Let me make myself more distinctly understood. We call this—you and I—a 'Working Men's' Institute, and our college in London, a 'Working Men's' College. Now, how do you consider that these several institutes differ, or ought to differ, from 'idle

men's' institutes, and 'idle men's' colleges? Or by what other word than 'idle' shall I distinguish those whom the happiest and wisest of working men do not object to call the 'Upper Classes?' Are there necessarily upper classes? necessarily lower? How much should those always be elevated, how much these always depressed? And I pray those among my audience who chance to occupy, at present, the higher position, to forgive me what offence there may be in what I am going to say. It is not *I* who wish to say it. Bitter voices say it; voices of battle and of famine through all the world, which must be heard some day, whoever keeps silence. Neither, as you well know, is it to *you* specially that I say it. I am sure that most now present know their duties of kindness, and fulfil them, better perhaps than I do mine. But I speak to you as representing your whole class, which errs, I know, chiefly by thoughtlessness, but not therefore the less terribly. Wilful error is limited by the will, but what limit is there to that of which we are unconscious?

19. Bear with me, therefore, while I turn to these workmen, and ask them, what they think the 'upper classes' are, and ought to be, in relation to them. Answer, you workmen who are here, as you would among yourselves, frankly; and tell me how you would have me call your employers. Am

I to call them—would *you* think me right in calling them—the idle classes? I think you would feel somewhat uneasy, and as if I were not treating my subject honestly, or speaking from my heart, if I proceeded in my lecture under the supposition that all rich people were idle. You would be both unjust and unwise if you allowed me to say that;—not less unjust than the rich people, who say that all the poor are idle, and will never work if they can help it, or more than they can help.

20.* For indeed the fact is, that there are idle poor, and idle rich; and there are busy poor, and busy rich. Many a beggar is as lazy as if he had ten thousand a year; and many a man of large fortune is busier than his errand-boy, and never would think of stopping in the street to play marbles. So that, in a large view, the distinction between workers and idlers, as between knaves and honest men, runs through the very heart and innermost nature of men of all ranks and in all positions. There is a working class—strong and happy,—among both rich and poor; there is an idle class—weak, wicked, and miserable,—among both rich and poor. And the worst of the misunderstandings arising between the

* Note this paragraph. I cannot enough wonder at the want of common charity which blinds so many people to the quite simple truth to which it refers.

two orders come of the unlucky fact that the wise of one class [how little wise in this !] habitually contemplate the foolish of the *other*. If the busy rich people watched and rebuked the idle rich people, all would be right among *them*: and if the busy poor people watched and rebuked the idle poor people, all would be right among *them*. But each look for the faults of the other. A hardworking man of property is particularly offended by an idle beggar; and an orderly, but poor, workman is naturally intolerant of the licentious luxury of the rich. And what is severe judgment in the minds of the just men of either class, becomes fierce enmity in the unjust—but among the unjust *only*. None but the dissolute among the poor look upon the rich as their natural enemies, or desire to pillage their houses and divide their property. None but the dissolute among the rich speak in opprobrious terms of the vices and follies of the poor.

21. There is, then, no worldly distinction between idle and industrious people; and I am going to-night to speak only of the industrious. The idle people we will put out of our thoughts at once—they are mere nuisances—what ought to be done with *them*, we'll talk of at another time. But there are class distinctions among the industrious themselves;—tremendous distinctions, which rise and fall to every degree in the

infinite thermometer of human pain and of human power,—distinctions of high and low, of lost and won, to the whole reach of man's soul and body.

22. These separations we will study, and the laws of them, among energetic men only, who, whether they work or whether they play, put their strength into the work, and their strength into the game; being in the full sense of the word 'industrious,' one way or another,—with purpose, or without. And these distinctions are mainly four:

I. Between those who work, and those who play.

II. Between those who produce the means of life, and those who consume them.

III. Between those who work with the head, and those who work with the hand.

IV. Between those who work wisely, and who work foolishly.

For easier memory, let us say we are going to oppose, in our examination,—

I. Work to play;

II. Production to consumption;

III. Head to hand; and,

IV. Sense to nonsense.

23. I. First, then, of the distinction between the classes who work and the classes who play. Of course we must agree upon a definition of these terms,—work and play, before going farther. Now,

roughly, not with vain subtlety of definition, but for plain use of the words, 'play' is an exertion of body or mind, made to please ourselves, and with no determined end; and work is a thing done because it ought to be done, and with a determined end. You play, as you call it, at cricket, for instance. That is as hard work as anything else; but it amuses you, and it has no result but the amusement. If it were done as an ordered form of exercise, for health's sake, it would become work directly. So, in like manner, whatever we do to please ourselves, and only for the sake of the pleasure, not for an ultimate object, is 'play,' the 'pleasing thing,' not the useful thing. Play may be useful, in a secondary sense; (nothing is indeed more useful or necessary); but the use of it depends on its being spontaneous.

24. Let us, then, enquire together what sort of games the playing class in England spend their lives in playing at.

The first of all English games is making money. That is an all-absorbing game; and we knock each other down oftener in playing at that, than at football, or any other roughest sport: and it is absolutely without purpose; no one who engages heartily in that game ever knows why. Ask a great money-maker what he wants to do with his money,—he never knows. He doesn't make it to do anything with it. He gets it only that he *may* get it. 'What will you make of what you have got?' you ask. 'Well, I'll get more,' he says. Just as, at cricket, you get more runs. There's no use in the runs, but to get more of them than other people is the game. And there's no use in the money, but to have more of it than other people is the game. So all that great foul city of London there,—rattling, growling, smoking, stinking, — a ghastly heap of fermenting brickwork, pouring out poison at every pore,—you fancy it is a city of work? Not a street of it! It is a great city of play; very nasty play, and very hard play, but still play. It is only Lord's cricket-ground without the turf:—a huge billiard-table without the cloth, and with pockets as deep as the bottomless pit; but mainly a billiard-table, after all.

25. Well, the first great English game is this playing at counters. It differs from the rest in that it appears always to be producing money, while every other game is expensive. But it does not always produce money. There's a great difference between 'winning' money and 'making' it: a great difference between getting it out of another man's pocket into ours, or filling both.

26. Our next great English games, however, hunting and shooting, are costly altogether; and how much we are fined for them annually in land, horses, gamekeepers, and game laws, and the resultant demoralization of ourselves, our children, and our retainers, I will not endeavour to count now; but note only that, except for exercise, this is not merely a useless game, but a deadly one, to all connected with it. For through horse-racing, you get every form of what the higher classes everywhere call 'Play,' in distinction from all other plays; that is, gambling; and through game-preserving, you get also some curious laying out of ground: that beautiful arrangement of dwelling-house for man and beast, by which we have grouse and blackcock—so many brace to the acre, and men and women—so many brace to the garret. I often wonder what the angelic builders and surveyors—the angelic builders who build the 'many mansions' up above there; and the angelic surveyors who measured that four-square city with their measuring reeds—I wonder what they think, or are supposed to think, of the laying out of ground by this nation.*

* The subject is pursued at some length in *Fors Clavigera* for March, 1873; but I have not yet properly stated the opposite side of the question, nor insisted on the value of uncultivated land to the national health of body and mind.

27. Then, next to the gentlemen's game of hunting, we must put the ladies' game of dressing. It is not the cheapest of games. And I wish I could tell you what this 'play' costs, altogether, in England, France, and Russia annually. But it is a pretty game, and on certain terms I like it; nay, I don't see it played quite as much as I would fain have it. You ladies like to lead the fashion:—by all means lead it—lead it thoroughly—lead it far enough. Dress yourselves nicely, and dress everybody else nicely. Lead the *fashions for the poor* first; make *them* look well, and you yourselves will look, in ways of which you have now no conception, all the better. The fashions you have set for some time among your peasantry are not pretty ones; their doublets are too irregularly slashed, or as Chaucer calls it "all to-slittered," though not "for queintise," and the wind blows too frankly through them.

28. Then there are other games, wild enough, as I could show you if I had time.

There's playing at literature, and playing at art;—very different, both, from working at literature, or working at art, but I've no time to speak of these. I pass to the greatest of all—the play of plays, the great gentlemen's game, which ladies like them best to play at,—the game of War. It is entrancingly pleasant to the imagination; we dress for it, however, more finely than for any other sport; and go out to it, not merely in scarlet, as to hunt, but in scarlet and gold, and all manner of fine colours: of course we could fight better in grey, and without feathers; but all nations have agreed that it is good to be well dressed at this play. Then the bats and balls are very costly; our English and French bats, with the balls and wickets, even those which we don't make any use of, costing, I suppose, now about fifteen millions of money annually to each nation; all which you know is paid for by hard labourer's work in the furrow and furnace. A costly game!—not to speak of its consequences; I will say at present nothing of these. The mere immediate cost of all these plays is what I want you to consider; they are all paid for in deadly work somewhere, as many of us know too well. The jewel-cutter, whose sight fails over the diamonds; the weaver, whose arm fails over the web; the iron-forger, whose breath fails before the furnace—*they* know what work is—they, who have all the work, and none of the play, except a kind they have named for themselves down in the black north country, where 'play' means being laid up by sickness. It is a pretty example for philologists, of varying dialect, this change in the sense of the word as used in the black country of Birmingham, and the red and black country of Baden Baden. Yes, gentlemen, and gentlewomen, of England, who think 'one moment unamused a misery, not made for feeble man,' this is what you have brought the word 'play' to mean, in the heart of merry England! You may have your fluting and piping; but there are sad children sitting in the market-place, who indeed cannot say to you, 'We have piped unto you, and ye have not danced:' but eternally shall say to you, 'We have mourned unto you, and ye have not lamented.'

29. This, then, is the first distinction between the 'upper and lower' classes. And this is one which is by no means necessary; which indeed must, in process of good time, be by all honest men's consent abolished. Men will be taught that an existence of play, sustained by the blood of other creatures, is a good existence for gnats and jelly-fish; but not for men: that neither days, nor lives, can be made holy or noble by doing nothing in them: that the best prayer at the beginning of a day is that we may not lose its moments; and the best grace before meat, the consciousness that we have justly earned our dinner. And when we have this much of plain Christianity preached to us again, and cease to translate the strict words, 'Son, go work to-day in my vineyard,' into the dainty ones, 'Baby, go play

to-day in my vineyard,' we shall all be workers in one way or another; and this much at least of the distinction between 'upper' and 'lower' forgotten.

30. II. I pass then to our second distinction; between the rich and poor, between Dives and Lazarus, — distinction which exists more sternly, I suppose, in this day, than ever in the world, Pagan or Christian, till now. Consider, for instance, what the general tenor of such a paper as the *Morning Post* implies of delicate luxury among the rich; and then read this chance extract from it:—

'Yesterday morning, at eight o'clock, a woman, passing a dung heap in the stone yard near the recently-erected almshouses in Shadwell Gap, High Street, Shadwell, called the attention of a Thames police-constable to a man in a sitting position on the dung heap, and said she was afraid he was dead. Her fears proved to be true. The wretched creature appeared to have been dead several hours. He had perished of cold and wet, and the rain had been beating down on him all night. The deceased was a bone-picker. He was in the lowest stage of poverty, poorly clad, and half-starved. The police had frequently driven him away from the stone yard, between sunset and sunrise, and told him to go home. He selected a most desolate spot for his wretched death. A penny and some bones were found in his pockets. The deceased was between fifty and sixty years of age. Inspector Roberts, of the K division, has given directions for inquiries to be made at the lodging-houses respecting the deceased, to ascertain his identity if possible.'—*Morning Post*, November 25, 1864.

Compare the statement of the finding bones in his pocket with the following, from the *Telegraph* of January 16 of this year:—

'Again, the dietary scale for adult and juvenile paupers was drawn up by the most conspicuous political economists in England. It is low in quantity, but it is sufficient to support nature; yet, within ten years of the passing of the Poor Law Act, we heard of the paupers in the Andover Union gnawing the scraps of putrid flesh, and sucking the marrow from the bones of horses which they were employed to crush.'

You see my reason for thinking that our Lazarus of Christianity has some advantage over the Jewish one. Jewish Lazarus expected, or, at least, prayed, to be fed with crumbs from the rich man's table; but *our* Lazarus is fed with crumbs from the dog's table.

31. Now this distinction between rich and poor rests on two bases. Within its proper limits, on a basis which is lawful and everlastingly necessary; beyond them, on a basis unlawful, and everlastingly corrupting the frame-work of society. The lawful

basis of wealth is, that a man who works should be paid the fair value of his work; and that if he does not choose to spend it to-day, he should have free leave to keep it, and spend it to-morrow. Thus, an industrious man working daily, and laying by daily, attains at last the possession of an accumulated sum of wealth, to which he has absolute right. The idle person who will not work, and the wasteful person who lays nothing by, at the end of the same time will be doubly poor—poor in possession, and dissolute in moral habit; and he will then naturally covet the money which the other has saved. And if he is then allowed to attack the other, and rob him of his well-earned wealth, there is no more any motive for saving, or any reward for good conduct; and all society is thereupon dissolved, or exists only in systems of rapine. Therefore the first necessity of social life is the clearness of national conscience in enforcing the law—that he should keep who has JUSTLY EARNED.

32. That law, I say, is the proper basis of distinction between rich and poor. But there is also a false basis of distinction; namely, the power held over those who are earning wealth by those who already possess it, and only use it to gain more. There will be always a number of men who would fain set themselves to the accumulation of wealth

as the sole object of their lives. Necessarily, that class of men is an uneducated class, inferior in intellect, and, more or less, cowardly. It is physically impossible for a well-educated, intellectual, or brave man to make money the chief object of his thoughts; just as it is for him to make his dinner the principal object of them. All healthy people like their dinners, but their dinner is not the main object of their lives. So all healthily-minded people like making money—ought to like it, and to enjoy the sensation of winning it: but the main object of their life is not money; it is something better than money. A good soldier, for instance, mainly wishes to do his fighting well. He is glad of his pay—very properly so, and justly grumbles when you keep him ten years without it—still, his main notion of life is to win battles, not to be paid for winning them. So of clergymen. They like pew-rents, and baptismal fees, of course; but yet, if they are brave and well educated, the pew-rent is not the sole object of their lives, and the baptismal fee is not the sole purpose of the baptism; the clergyman's object is essentially to baptize and preach, not to be paid for preaching. So of doctors. They like fees no doubt,—ought to like them; yet if they are brave and well educated, the entire object of their lives is not fees. They, on the whole, desire to cure the sick; and,—if they are good doctors, and the choice were fairly put to them—would rather cure their patient, and lose their fee, than kill him, and get it. And so with all other brave and rightly-trained men; their work is first, their fee second—very important always, but still *second*. But in every nation, as I said, there are a vast class who are ill-educated, cowardly, and more or less stupid. And with these people, just as certainly the fee is first, and the work second, as with brave people the work is first, and the fee second. And this is no small distinction. It is between life and death *in* a man; between heaven and hell *for* him. You cannot serve two masters;—you *must* serve one or other. If your work is first with you, and your fee second, work is your master, and the lord of work, who is God. But if your fee is first with you, and your work second, fee is your master, and the lord of fee, who is the Devil; and not only the Devil, but the lowest of devils—the 'least erected fiend that fell.' So there you have it in brief terms; Work first—you are God's servants; Fee first—you are the Fiend's. And it makes a difference, now and ever, believe me, whether you serve Him who has on His vesture and thigh written, 'King of Kings,' and whose service is perfect freedom; or him on whose vesture and thigh the name is written, 'Slave of Slaves,' and whose service is perfect slavery.

33. However, in every nation there are, and must always be, a certain number of these Fiend's servants, who have it principally for the object of their lives to make money. They are always, as I said, more or less stupid, and cannot conceive of anything else so nice as money. Stupidity is always the basis of the Judas bargain. We do great injustice to Iscariot, in thinking him wicked above all common wickedness. He was only a common money-lover, and, like all money-lovers, did not understand Christ;—could not make out the worth of Him, or meaning of Him. He never thought He would be killed. He was horror-struck when he found that Christ would be killed; threw his money away instantly, and hanged himself. How many of our present money-seekers, think you, would have the grace to hang themselves, whoever was killed? But Judas was a common, selfish, muddle-headed, pilfering fellow; his hand always in the bag of the poor, not caring for them. Helpless to understand Christ, he yet believed in Him, much more than most of us do; had seen Him do miracles, thought He was quite strong enough to shift for Himself, and he, Judas, might as well make his own little bye-perquisites out of the affair. Christ would come out of it well enough, and he have his thirty pieces. Now, that is the money-seeker's idea, all over the world. He doesn't hate Christ, but can't

understand Him—doesn't care for Him—sees no good in that benevolent business; makes his own little job out of it at all events, come what will. And thus, out of every mass of men, you have a certain number of bagmen—your 'fee-first' men, whose main object is to make money. And they do make it—make it in all sorts of unfair ways, chiefly by the weight and force of money itself, or what is called the power of capital; that is to say, the power which money, once obtained, has over the labour of the poor, so that the capitalist can take all its produce to himself, except the labourer's food. That is the modern Judas's way of 'carrying the bag,' and 'bearing what is put therein.'

34. Nay, but (it is asked) how is that an unfair advantage? Has not the man who has worked for the money a right to use it as he best can? No; in this respect, money is now exactly what mountain promontories over public roads were in old times. The barons fought for them fairly:—the strongest and cunningest got them; then fortified them, and made every one who passed below pay toll. Well, capital now is exactly what crags were then. Men fight fairly (we will, at least, grant so much, though it is more than we ought) for their money: but, once having got it, the fortified millionaire can make everybody who passes below pay toll to his million,

and build another tower of his money castle. And I can tell you, the poor vagrants by the roadside suffer now quite as much from the bag-baron, as ever they did from the crag-baron. Bags and crags have just the same result on rags. I have not time, however, to-night, to show you in how many ways the power of capital is unjust: but remember this one great principle—you will find it unfailing—that whenever money is the principal object of life with either man or nation, it is both got ill, and spent ill; and does harm both in the getting and spending; but when it is not the principal object, it and all other things will be well got, and well spent. And here is the test, with every man, whether money is the principal object with him, or not. If in mid-life he could pause and say, 'Now I have enough to live upon, I'll live upon it; and having well earned it, I will also well spend it, and go out of the world poor, as I came into it,' then money is not principal with him; but if, having enough to live upon in the manner befitting his character and rank, he still wants to make more, and to *die* rich, then money is the principal object with him, and it becomes a curse to himself, and generally to those who spend it after him. For you know it *must* be spent some day; the only question is whether the man who makes it shall spend it, or some one else; and generally it is better for the maker to spend it, for he will know best its value and use. And if a man does not choose thus to spend his money, he must either hoard it or lend it, and the worst thing he can generally do is to lend it; for borrowers are nearly always ill-spenders, and it is with lent money that all evil is mainly done, and all unjust war protracted.

35. For observe what the real fact is, respecting loans to foreign military governments, and how strange it is. If your little boy came to you to ask for money to spend in squibs and crackers, you would think twice before you gave it him: and you would have some idea that it was wasted, when you saw it fly off in fireworks, even though he did no mischief with it. But the Russian children, and Austrian children, come to you, borrowing money, not to spend in innocent squibs, but in cartridges and bayonets to attack you in India with, and to keep down all noble life in Italy with, and to murder Polish women and children with; and *that* you will give at once, because they pay you interest for it. Now, in order to pay you that interest, they must tax every working peasant in their dominions; and on that work you live. You therefore at once rob the Austrian peasant, assassinate or banish the Polish peasant, and you

live on the produce of the theft, and the bribe for the assassination! That is the broad fact—that is the practical meaning of your foreign loans, and of most large interest of money; and then you quarrel with Bishop Colenso, forsooth, as if *he* denied the Bible, and you believed it! though every deliberate act of your lives is a new defiance of its primary orders.

36. III. I must pass, however, now to our third condition of separation, between the men who work with the hand, and those who work with the head.

And here we have at last an inevitable distinction. There *must* be work done by the arms, or none of us could live. There *must* be work done by the brains, or the life we get would not be worth having. And the same men cannot do both. There is rough work to be done, and rough men must do it; there is gentle work to be done, and gentlemen must do it; and it is physically impossible that one class should do, or divide, the work of the other. And it is of no use to try to conceal this sorrowful fact by fine words, and to talk to the workman about the honourableness of manual labour, and the dignity of humanity. Rough work, honourable or not, takes the life out of us; and the man who has been heaving clay out of a ditch all day, or driving an express train against the north wind all night, or holding a collier's helm in a gale on a lee shore, or whirling white-hot iron at a furnace mouth, is not the same man at the end of his day, or night, as one who has been sitting in a quiet room, with everything comfortable about him, reading books, or classing butterflies, or painting pictures.* If it is any comfort to you to be told that the rough work is the more honourable of the two, I should be sorry to take that much of consolation from you; and in some sense I need not. The rough work is at all events real, honest, and, generally, though not always, useful; while the fine work is, a great deal of it, foolish and false, as well as fine, and therefore dishonourable; but when both kinds are equally well and worthily done, the head's is the noble work, and the hand's the ignoble. Therefore, of all hand work whatsoever, necessary for the maintenance of life, those old words, 'In the sweat of thy face thou shalt eat bread,' indicate that the inherent nature of it is one of calamity; and that the ground, cursed for our sake, casts also some shadow of degradation into our contest with its thorn and its thistle; so that all nations have held their days honourable, or 'holy,' and constituted them 'holydays,' or 'holidays,' by making them days of rest; and the promise, which,

* Compare § 57.

among all our distant hopes, seems to cast the chief brightness over death, is that blessing of the dead who die in the Lord, that 'they rest from their labours, and their works do follow them.'

37. And thus the perpetual question and contest must arise, who is to do this rough work? and how is the worker of it to be comforted, redeemed, and rewarded? and what kind of play should he have, and what rest, in this world, sometimes, as well as in the next? Well, my good, laborious, friends, these questions will take a little time to answer yet. They *must* be answered: all good men are occupied with them, and all honest thinkers. There's grand head work doing about them; but much must be discovered, and much attempted in vain, before anything decisive can be told you. Only note these few particulars, which are already sure.

38. As to the distribution of the hard work. None of us, or very few of us, do either hard or soft work because we think we ought; but because we have chanced to fall into the way of it, and cannot help ourselves. Now, nobody does anything well that they cannot help doing: work is only done well when it is done with a will; and no man has a thoroughly sound will unless he knows he is doing what he should, and is in his place. And, depend upon it, all work must be done at last, not in a dis-

orderly, scrambling, doggish way, but in an ordered, soldierly, human way—a lawful or 'loyal' way. Men are enlisted for the labour that kills—the labour of war: they are counted, trained, fed, dressed, and praised for that. Let them be enlisted also for the labour that feeds: let them be counted, trained, fed, dressed, praised for that. Teach the plough exercise as carefully as you do the sword exercise, and let the officers of troops of life be held as much gentlemen as the officers of troops of death; and all is done: but neither this, nor any other right thing, can be accomplished—you can't even see your way to it—unless, first of all, both servant and master are resolved that, come what will of it, they will do each other justice.

39. People are perpetually squabbling about what will be best to do, or easiest to do, or adviseablest to do, or profitablest to do; but they never, so far as I hear them talk, ever ask what it is *just* to do. And it is the law of heaven that you shall not be able to judge what is wise or easy, unless you are first resolved to judge what is just, and to do it. That is the one thing constantly reiterated by our Master—the order of all others that is given oftenest—'Do justice and judgment.' That's your Bible order; that's the 'Service of God,'—not praying nor psalm-singing.

You are told, indeed, to sing psalms when you are merry, and to pray when you need anything; and, by the perverseness of the evil Spirit in us, we get to think that praying and psalm-singing are 'service.' If a child finds itself in want of anything, it runs in and asks its father for it—does it call that doing its father a service? If it begs for a toy or a piece of cake—does it call that serving its father? That, with God, is prayer, and He likes to hear it: He likes you to ask Him for cake when you want it; but He doesn't call that 'serving Him.' Begging is not serving: God likes mere beggars as little as you do—He likes honest servants,—not beggars. So when a child loves its father very much, and is very happy, it may sing little songs about him; but it doesn't call that, serving its father; neither is singing songs about God, serving God. It is enjoying ourselves, if it's anything; most probably it is nothing: but if it's anything, it is serving ourselves, not God. And yet we are impudent enough to call our beggings and chauntings 'Divine Service:' we say, 'Divine service will be "performed"' (that's our word—the form of it gone through) 'at so-and-so o'clock.' Alas! unless we perform Divine service in every willing act of life, we never perform it at all. The one Divine work—the one ordered sacrifice—is to do justice; and it is the last we are ever inclined to do. Anything rather than that! As much charity as you choose, but no justice. 'Nay,' you will say, 'charity is greater than justice.' Yes, it is greater; it is the summit of justice —it is the temple of which justice is the foundation. But you can't have the top without the bottom; you cannot build upon charity. You must build upon justice, for this main reason, that you have not, at first, charity to build with. It is the last reward of good work. Do justice to your brother (you can do that, whether you love him or not), and you will come to love him. But do injustice to him, because you don't love him; and you will come to hate him.

40. It is all very fine to think you can build upon charity to begin with; but you will find all you have got to begin with begins at home, and is essentially love of yourself. You well-to-do people, for instance, who are here to-night, will go to 'Divine service' next Sunday, all nice and tidy; and your little children will have their tight little Sunday boots on, and lovely little Sunday feathers in their hats; and you'll think, complacently and piously, how lovely they look going to church in their best! So they do: and you love them heartily, and you like sticking feathers in their hats. That's all right: that *is* charity; but it is charity beginning at home. Then you will come to the poor little crossing-sweeper, got up also,— it in its Sunday dress,—the dirtiest rags it has,—that

it may beg the better: you will give it a penny, and think how good you are, and how good God is to prefer *your* child to the crossing-sweeper, and bestow on it a divine hat, feather, and boots, and the pleasure of giving pence, instead of begging for them. That's charity going abroad. But what does Justice say, walking and watching near us? Christian Justice has been strangely mute and seemingly blind; and, if not blind, decrepit, this many a day: she keeps her accounts still, however—quite steadily—doing them at nights, carefully, with her bandage off, and through acutest spectacles (the only modern scientific invention she cares about). You must put your ear down ever so close to her lips, to hear her speak; and then you will start at what she first whispers, for it will certainly be, 'Why shouldn't that little crossing-sweeper have a feather on its head, as well as your own child?' Then you may ask Justice, in an amazed manner, 'How she can possibly be so foolish as to think children could sweep crossings with feathers on their heads?' Then you stoop again, and Justice says—still in her dull, stupid way—'Then, why don't you, every other Sunday, leave your child to sweep the crossing, and take the little sweeper to church in a hat and feather?' Mercy on us (you think), what will she say next! And you answer, of course, that 'you don't, because everybody ought to remain content in the position in which Providence has placed them.' Ah, my friends, that's the gist of the whole question. *Did* Providence put them in that position, or did *you?* You knock a man into a ditch, and then you tell him to remain content in the 'position in which Providence has placed him.' That's modern Christianity. You say—'*We* did not knock him into the ditch.' We shall never know what you have done, or left undone, until the question with us, every morning, is, not how to do the gainful thing, but how to do the just thing, during the day; nor until we are at least so far on the way to being Christian, as to acknowledge that maxim of the poor half-way Mahometan, 'One hour in the execution of justice is worth seventy years of prayer.'

41. Supposing, then, we have it determined with appropriate justice, *who* is to do the hand work, the next questions must be how the hand-workers are to be paid, and how they are to be refreshed, and what play they are to have. Now, the possible quantity of play depends on the possible quantity of pay; and the quantity of pay is not a matter for consideration to hand-workers only, but to all workers. Generally, good, useful work, whether of the hand or head, is either ill-paid, or not paid at all. I don't say it should be so, but it always is so.

4

People, as a rule, only pay for being amused or being cheated, not for being served. Five thousand a year to your talker, and a shilling a day to your fighter, digger, and thinker, is the rule. None of the best head work in art, literature, or science, is ever paid for. How much do you think Homer got for his *Iliad?* or Dante for his *Paradise?* only bitter bread and salt, and going up and down other people's stairs. In science, the man who discovered the telescope, and first saw heaven, was paid with a dungeon; the man who invented the microscope, and first saw earth, died of starvation, driven from his home. It is indeed very clear that God means all thoroughly good work and talk to be done for nothing. Baruch the scribe did not get a penny a line for writing Jeremiah's second roll for him, I fancy; and St. Stephen did not get bishop's pay for that long sermon of his to the Pharisees; nothing but stones. For indeed that is the world-father's proper payment. So surely as any of the world's children work for the world's good, honestly, with head and heart; and come to it, saying, 'Give us a little bread, just to keep the life in us,' the world-father answers them, 'No, my children, not bread; a stone, if you like, or as many as you need, to keep you quiet, and tell to future ages, how unpleasant you made yourself to the one you lived in.'

42. But the hand-workers are not so ill off as all this comes to. The worst that can happen to *you* is to break stones; not be broken by them. And for you there will come a time for better payment; some day, assuredly, we shall pay people not quite so much for talking in Parliament and doing nothing, as for holding their tongues out of it, and doing something; we shall pay our ploughman a little more, and our lawyer a little less, and so on: but, at least, we may even now take care that whatever work is done shall be fully paid for; and the man who does it, paid for it, not somebody else; and that it shall be done in an orderly, soldierly, well-guided, wholesome way, under good captains and lieutenants of labour; and that it shall have its appointed times of rest, and enough of them; and that, in those times, the play shall be wholesome play, not in theatrical gardens, with tin flowers and gas sunshine, and girls dancing because of their misery; but in true gardens, with real flowers, and real sunshine, and children dancing because of their gladness; so that truly the streets shall be full (the 'streets,' mind you, not the gutters,) of children, playing in the midst thereof. We may take care that working men shall have at least as good books to read as anybody else, when they've time to read them; and as comfortable firesides

to sit at as anybody else, when they've time to sit at them. This, I think, can be managed for you, my laborious friends, in the good time.

43. IV. I must go on, however, to our last head, concerning ourselves all, as workers. What is wise work, and what is foolish work? What the difference between sense and nonsense, in daily occupation?

There are three tests of wise work:—that it must be honest, useful, and cheerful.

I. It is HONEST. I hardly know anything more strange than that you recognize honesty in play, and you do not in work. In your lightest games, you have always some one to see what you call 'fair-play.' In boxing, you must hit fair; in racing, start fair. Your English watchword is 'fair-*play*,' your English hatred, foul-play. Did it never strike you that you wanted another watchword also, 'fair-*work*,' and another and bitterer hatred,—foul-*work?* Your prizefighter has some honour in him yet; and so have the men in the ring round him: they will judge him to lose the match, by foul hitting. But your prize-merchant gains his match by foul selling, and no one cries out against that! You drive a gambler out of the gambling-room who loads dice, but you leave a tradesman in flourishing business, who loads scales! For observe, all dishonest dealing *is* loading scales. What difference does it make whether I get short weight, adulterate substance, or dishonest fabric—unless that flaw in the substance or fabric is the worse evil of the two? Give me short measure of food, and I only lose by you; but give me adulterate food, and I die by you.

Here, then, is your chief duty, you workmen and tradesmen,—to be true to yourselves, and to us who would help you. We can do nothing for you, nor you for yourselves, without honesty. Get that, you get all; without that, your suffrages, your reforms, your free-trade measures, your institutions of science, are all in vain. It is useless to put your heads together, if you can't put your hearts together. Shoulder to shoulder, right hand to right hand, among yourselves, and no wrong hand to anybody else, and you'll win the world yet.

44. II. Then, secondly, wise work is USEFUL. No man minds, or ought to mind, its being hard, if only it comes to something; but when it is hard, and comes to nothing; when all our bees' business turns to spiders'; and for honey-comb we have only resultant cobweb, blown away by the next breeze,—that is the cruel thing for the worker. Yet do we ever ask ourselves, personally, or even nationally, whether our work is coming to anything or not? We don't care to keep what has been nobly done;

still less do we care to do nobly what others would keep; and, least of all, to make the work itself useful, instead of deadly, to the doer, so as to exert his life indeed, but not to waste it. Of all wastes, the greatest waste that you can commit is the waste of labour. If you went down in the morning into your dairy, and found that your youngest child had got down before you; and that he and the cat were at play together, and that he had poured out all the cream on the floor for the cat to lap up, you would scold the child, and be sorry the cream was wasted. But if, instead of wooden bowls with milk in them, there are golden bowls with human life in them, and instead of the cat to play with,—the devil to play with; and you yourself the player; and instead of leaving that golden bowl to be broken by God at the fountain, you break it in the dust yourself, and pour the human life out on the ground for the fiend to lick up—that is no waste!

45. What! you perhaps think, 'to waste the labour of men is not to kill them.' Is it not? I should like to know how you could kill them more utterly,—kill them with second deaths, seventh deaths, hundredfold deaths? It is the slightest way of killing to stop a man's breath. Nay, the hunger, and the cold, and the whistling bullets—our love messengers between nation and nation,—have

brought pleasant messages to many a man before now: orders of sweet release, and leave at last to go where he will be most welcome and most happy. At the worst you do but shorten his life, you do not corrupt his life. But if you put him to base labour, if you bind his thoughts, if you blind his eyes, if you blunt his hopes, if you steal his joys, if you stunt his body, and blast his soul, and at last leave him not so much as strength to reap the poor fruit of his degradation, but gather that for yourself, and dismiss him to the grave, when you have done with him, having, so far as in you lay, made the walls of that grave everlasting: (though, indeed, I fancy the goodly bricks of some of our family vaults will hold closer in the resurrection day than the sod over the labourer's head), this you think is no waste, and no sin!

46. IV. Then, lastly, wise work is CHEERFUL, as a child's work is. And now I want you to take one thought home with you, and let it stay with you.

Everybody in this room has been taught to pray daily, 'Thy kingdom come.' Now, if we hear a man swear in the streets, we think it very wrong, and say he 'takes God's name in vain.' But there's a twenty times worse way of taking His name in vain than that. It is to *ask God for what we don't want.* He doesn't like that sort of prayer. If you don't want a thing, don't ask for it: such asking is the worst mockery of your King you can insult Him with; the soldiers striking Him on the head with the reed was nothing to that. If you do not wish for His kingdom, don't pray for it. But if you do, you must do more than pray for it; you must work for it. And, to work for it, you must know what it is: we have all prayed for it many a day without thinking. Observe, it is a kingdom that is to come to us; we are not to go to it. Also, it is not to be a kingdom of the dead, but of the living. Also, it is not to come all at once, but quietly; nobody knows how. 'The kingdom of God cometh not with observation.' Also, it is not to come outside of us, but in our hearts: 'the kingdom of God is within you.' And, being within us, it is not a thing to be seen, but to be felt; and though it brings all substance of good with it, it does not consist in that: 'the kingdom of God is not meat and drink, but righteousness, peace, and joy in the Holy Ghost;' joy, that is to say, in the holy, healthful, and helpful Spirit. Now, if we want to work for this kingdom, and to bring it, and enter into it, there's one curious condition to be first accepted. You must enter it as children, or not at all: 'Whosoever will not receive it as a little child shall not enter therein.' And again, 'Suffer little children to come unto me, and forbid them not, *for of such is the kingdom of heaven.*'*

47. *Of such,* observe. Not of children themselves, but of such as children. I believe most mothers who read that text think that all heaven or the earth—when it gets to be like heaven—is to be full of babies. But that's not so. 'Length of days and long life and peace,' that is the blessing, not to die, still less to live, in babyhood. It is the *character* of children we want, and must gain at our peril; let us see, briefly, in what it consists.

The first character of right childhood is that it is Modest. A well-bred child does not think it can teach its parents, or that it knows everything. It may think its father and mother know everything, —perhaps that all grown-up people know everything; very certainly it is sure that *it* does not. And it is always asking questions, and wanting to know more. Well, that is the first character of a good and wise man at his work. To know that he knows very little;—to perceive that there are many above him wiser than he; and to be always asking questions, wanting to learn, not to teach. No one ever teaches well who wants to teach, or governs well who wants to govern; it is an old saying

* [I have referred oftener to the words of the English Bible in this lecture than in any other of my addresses, because I was here speaking to an audience which professed to accept its authority implicitly.]

(Plato's, but I know not if his, first), and as wise as old.

48. Then, the second character of right childhood is to be Faithful. Perceiving that its father knows best what is good for it, and having found always, when it has tried its own way against his, that he was right and it was wrong, a noble child trusts him at last wholly, gives him its hand, and will walk blindfold with him, if he bids it. And that is the true character of all good men also, as obedient workers, or soldiers under captains. They must trust their captains;—they are bound for their lives to choose none but those whom they *can* trust. Then, they are not always to be thinking that what seems strange to them, or wrong in what they are desired to do, *is* strange or wrong. They know their captain: where he leads they must follow, what he bids, they must do; and without this trust and faith, without this captainship and soldiership, no great deed, no great salvation, is possible to man.

49. Then, the third character of right childhood is to be Loving. Give a little love to a child, and you get a great deal back. It loves everything near it, when it is a right kind of child; would hurt nothing, would give the best it has away, always, if you need it; does not lay plans for getting everything in the house for itself: and, above all,

delights in helping people; you cannot please it so much as by giving it a chance of being useful, in ever so humble a way.

50. And because of all these characters, lastly, it is Cheerful. Putting its trust in its father, it is careful for nothing—being full of love to every creature, it is happy always, whether in its play or its duty. Well, that's the great worker's character also. Taking no thought for the morrow; taking thought only for the duty of the day; trusting somebody else to take care of to-morrow; knowing indeed what labour is, but not what sorrow is; and always ready for play—beautiful play. For lovely human play is like the play of the Sun. There's a worker for you. He, steady to his time, is set as a strong man to run his course, but also he *rejoiceth* as a strong man to run his course. See how he plays in the morning, with the mists below, and the clouds above, with a ray here, and a flash there, and a shower of jewels everywhere;—that's the Sun's play; and great human play is like his—all various—all full of light and life, and tender, as the dew of the morning.

51. So then, you have the child's character in these four things—Humility, Faith, Charity, and Cheerfulness. That's what you have got to be converted to. 'Except ye be converted and become as little children'—You hear much of conversion now-a-

days: but people always seem to think they have got to be made wretched by conversion,—to be converted to long faces. No, friends, you have got to be converted to short ones; you have to repent into childhood, to repent into delight, and delightsomeness. You can't go into a conventicle but you'll hear plenty of talk of backsliding. Backsliding, indeed! I can tell you, on the ways most of us go, the faster we slide back the better. Slide back into the cradle, if going on is into the grave: —back, I tell you; back—out of your long faces, and into your long clothes. It is among children only, and as children only, that you will find medicine for your healing and true wisdom for your teaching. There is poison in the counsels of the *men* of this world; the words they speak are all bitterness, 'the poison of asps is under their lips,' but 'the sucking child shall play by the hole of the asp.' There is death in the looks of men. 'Their eyes are privily set against the poor:' they are as the uncharmable serpent, the cockatrice, which slew by seeing. But 'the weaned child shall lay his hand on the cockatrice den.' There is death in the steps of men: 'their feet are swift to shed blood; they have compassed us in our steps like the lion that is greedy of his prey, and the young lion lurking in secret places;' but, in that kingdom, the wolf shall lie down with the lamb, and the fatling with the lion, and 'a little child shall lead them.' There is death in the thoughts of men: the world is one wide riddle to them, darker and darker as it draws to a close; but the secret of it is known to the child, and the Lord of heaven and earth is most to be thanked in that 'He has hidden these things from the wise and prudent, and has revealed them unto babes.' Yes, and there is death—infinitude of death—in the principalities and powers of men. As far as the east is from the west, so far our sins are —*not* set from us, but multiplied around us: the Sun himself, think you he *now* 'rejoices' to run his course, when he plunges westward to the horizon, so widely red, not with clouds, but blood? And it will be red more widely yet. Whatever drought of the early and latter rain may be, there will be none of that red rain. You fortify yourselves, you arm yourselves against it, in vain; the enemy and avenger will be upon you also, unless you learn that it is not out of the mouths of the knitted gun, or the smoothed rifle, but 'out of the mouths of babes and sucklings' that the strength is ordained, which shall 'still the enemy and avenger.'

LECTURE II.

TRAFFIC.

(*Delivered in the Town Hall, Bradford.*)

52. MY good Yorkshire friends, you asked me down here among your hills that I might talk to you about this Exchange you are going to build: but earnestly and seriously asking you to pardon me, I am going to do nothing of the kind. I cannot talk, or at least can say very little, about this same Exchange. I must talk of quite other things, though not willingly;—I could not deserve your pardon, if, when you invited me to speak on one subject, I *wilfully* spoke on another. But I cannot speak, to purpose, of anything about which I do not care; and most simply and sorrowfully I have to tell you, in the outset, that I do *not* care about this Exchange of yours.

If, however, when you sent me your invitation, I had answered, 'I won't come, I don't care about the Exchange of Bradford,' you would have been justly offended with me, not knowing the reasons of so blunt a carelessness. So I have come down, hoping that you will patiently let me tell you why, on this, and many other such occasions, I now remain silent, when formerly I should have caught at the opportunity of speaking to a gracious audience.

53. In a word, then, I do not care about this Exchange,—because *you* don't; and because you know perfectly well I cannot make you. Look at the essential conditions of the case, which you, as business men, know perfectly well, though perhaps you think I forget them. You are going to spend 30,000*l.*, which to you, collectively, is nothing; the buying a new coat is, as to the cost of it, a much more important matter of consideration, to me, than building a new Exchange is to you. But you think you may as well have the right thing for your money. You know there are a great many odd styles of architecture about; you don't want to do anything ridiculous; you hear of me, among others, as a respectable architectural man-milliner; and you send for me, that I may tell you the leading fashion; and what is, in our shops, for the moment, the newest and sweetest thing in pinnacles.

54. Now, pardon me for telling you frankly, you

cannot have good architecture merely by asking people's advice on occasion. All good architecture is the expression of national life and character; and it is produced by a prevalent and eager national taste, or desire for beauty. And I want you to think a little of the deep significance of this word 'taste;' for no statement of mine has been more earnestly or oftener controverted than that good taste is essentially a moral quality. 'No,' say many of my antagonists, 'taste is one thing, morality is another. Tell us what is pretty: we shall be glad to know that; but we need no sermons, even were you able to preach them, which may be doubted.'

Permit me, therefore, to fortify this old dogma of mine somewhat. Taste is not only a part and an index of morality;—it is the ONLY morality. The first, and last, and closest trial question to any living creature is, 'What do you like?' Tell me what you like, and I'll tell you what you are. Go out into the street, and ask the first man or woman you meet, what their 'taste' is; and if they answer candidly, you know them, body and soul. 'You, my friend in the rags, with the unsteady gait, what do *you* like?' 'A pipe, and a quartern of gin.' I know you. 'You, good woman, with the quick step and tidy bonnet, what do you like?' 'A swept hearth, and a clean tea-table; and my husband opposite me, and a baby at my breast.' Good, I know you also. 'You, little girl with the golden hair and the soft eyes, what do you like?' 'My canary, and a run among the wood hyacinths.' 'You, little boy with the dirty hands, and the low forehead, what do you like?' 'A shy at the sparrows, and a game at pitch-farthing.' Good; we know them all now. What more need we ask?

55. 'Nay,' perhaps you answer; 'we need rather to ask what these people and children do, than what they like. If they *do* right, it is no matter that they like what is wrong; and if they *do* wrong, it is no matter that they like what is right. Doing is the great thing; and it does not matter that the man likes drinking, so that he does not drink; nor that the little girl likes to be kind to her canary, if she will not learn her lessons; nor that the little boy likes throwing stones at the sparrows, if he goes to the Sunday school.' Indeed, for a short time, and in a provisional sense, this is true. For if, resolutely, people do what is right, in time they come to like doing it. But they only are in a right moral state when they *have* come to like doing it; and as long as they don't like it, they are still in a vicious state. The man is not in health of body who is always thinking of the bottle in the cupboard, though he bravely bears his thirst; but the man who heartily

enjoys water in the morning, and wine in the evening, each in its proper quantity and time. And the entire object of true education is to make people not merely *do* the right things, but *enjoy* the right things: —not merely industrious, but to love industry—not merely learned, but to love knowledge—not merely pure, but to love purity—not merely just, but to hunger and thirst after justice.

56. But you may answer or think, 'Is the liking for outside ornaments,—for pictures, or statues, or furniture, or architecture,—a moral quality?' Yes, most surely, if a rightly set liking. Taste for *any* pictures or statues is not a moral quality, but taste for good ones is. Only here again we have to define the word 'good.' I don't mean by 'good,' clever —or learned—or difficult in the doing. Take a picture by Teniers, of sots quarrelling over their dice: it is an entirely clever picture; so clever that nothing in its kind has ever been done equal to it; but it is also an entirely base and evil picture. It is an expression of delight in the prolonged contemplation of a vile thing, and delight in that is an 'unmannered,' or 'immoral' quality. It is 'bad taste' in the profoundest sense—it is the taste of the devils. On the other hand, a picture of Titian's, or a Greek statue, or a Greek coin, or a Turner landscape, expresses delight in the perpetual contempla-

tion of a good and perfect thing. That is an entirely moral quality—it is the taste of the angels. And all delight in fine art, and all love of it, resolve themselves into simple love of that which deserves love. That deserving is the quality which we call 'loveliness'—(we ought to have an opposite word, hateliness, to be said of the things which deserve to be hated); and it is not an indifferent nor optional thing whether we love this or that; but it is just the vital function of all our being. What we *like* determines what we *are*, and is the sign of what we are; and to teach taste is inevitably to form character.

57. As I was thinking over this, in walking up Fleet Street the other day, my eye caught the title of a book standing open in a bookseller's window. It was—'On the necessity of the diffusion of taste among all classes.' 'Ah,' I thought to myself, 'my classifying friend, when you have diffused your taste, where will your classes be? The man who likes what you like, belongs to the same class with you, I think. Inevitably so. You may put him to other work if you choose; but, by the condition you have brought him into, he will dislike the work as much as you would yourself. You get hold of a scavenger or a costermonger, who enjoyed the Newgate Calendar for literature, and

"Pop goes the Weasel" for music. You think you can make him like Dante and Beethoven? I wish you joy of your lessons; but if you do, you have made a gentleman of him:—he won't like to go back to his costermongering.'

58. And so completely and unexceptionally is this so, that, if I had time to-night, I could show you that a nation cannot be affected by any vice, or weakness, without expressing it, legibly, and for ever, either in bad art, or by want of art; and that there is no national virtue, small or great, which is not manifestly expressed in all the art which circumstances enable the people possessing that virtue to produce. Take, for instance, your great English virtue of enduring and patient courage. You have at present in England only one art of any consequence—that is, iron-working. You know thoroughly well how to cast and hammer iron. Now, do you think, in those masses of lava which you build volcanic cones to melt, and which you forge at the mouths of the Infernos you have created; do you think, on those iron plates, your courage and endurance are not written for ever,—not merely with an iron pen, but on iron parchment? And take also your great English vice—European vice—vice of all the world—vice of all other worlds that roll or shine in heaven, bearing with them yet the

atmosphere of hell—the vice of jealousy, which brings competition into your commerce, treachery into your councils, and dishonour into your wars—that vice which has rendered for you, and for your next neighbouring nation, the daily occupations of existence no longer possible, but with the mail upon your breasts and the sword loose in its sheath; so that, at last, you have realized for all the multitudes of the two great peoples who lead the so-called civilization of the earth,—you have realized for them all, I say, in person and in policy, what was once true only of the rough Border riders of your Cheviot hills—

'They carved at the meal
With gloves of steel,
And they drank the red wine through the helmet barr'd;'—

do you think that this national shame and dastardliness of heart are not written as legibly on every rivet of your iron armour as the strength of the right hands that forged it?

59. Friends, I know not whether this thing be the more ludicrous or the more melancholy. It is quite unspeakably both. Suppose, instead of being now sent for by you, I had been sent for by some private gentleman, living in a suburban house, with his garden separated only by a fruit-wall from his next door neighbour's; and he had

called me to consult with him on the furnishing of his drawing-room. I begin looking about me, and find the walls rather bare; I think such and such a paper might be desirable—perhaps a little fresco here and there on the ceiling—a damask curtain or so at the windows. 'Ah,' says my employer, 'damask curtains, indeed! That's all very fine, but you know I can't afford that kind of thing just now!' 'Yet the world credits you with a splendid income!' 'Ah, yes,' says my friend, 'but do you know, at present, I am obliged to spend it nearly all in steel-traps?' 'Steel-traps! for whom?' 'Why, for that fellow on the other side the wall, you know: we're very good friends, capital friends; but we are obliged to keep our traps set on both sides of the wall; we could not possibly keep on friendly terms without them, and our spring guns. The worst of it is, we are both clever fellows enough; and there's never a day passes that we don't find out a new trap, or a new gun-barrel, or something; we spend about fifteen millions a year each in our traps, take it all together; and I don't see how we're to do with less.' A highly comic state of life for two private gentlemen! but for two nations, it seems to me, not wholly comic. Bedlam would be comic, perhaps, if there were only one madman in it; and your Christmas pantomime is comic, when there is only one clown in it; but when the whole world turns clown, and paints itself red with its own heart's blood instead of vermilion, it is something else than comic, I think.

60. Mind, I know a great deal of this is play, and willingly allow for that. You don't know what to do with yourselves for a sensation: fox-hunting and cricketing will not carry you through the whole of this unendurably long mortal life: you liked popguns when you were schoolboys, and rifles and Armstrongs are only the same things better made: but then the worst of it is, that what was play to you when boys, was not play to the sparrows; and what is play to you now, is not play to the small birds of State neither; and for the black eagles, you are somewhat shy of taking shots at them, if I mistake not.

61. I must get back to the matter in hand, however. Believe me, without farther instance, I could show you, in all time, that every nation's vice, or virtue, was written in its art: the soldiership of early Greece; the sensuality of late Italy; the visionary religion of Tuscany; the splendid human energy of Venice. I have no time to do this to-night (I have done it elsewhere before now); but I proceed to apply the principle to ourselves in a more searching manner.

I notice that among all the new buildings which

cover your once wild hills, churches and schools are mixed in due, that is to say, in large proportion, with your mills and mansions; and I notice also that the churches and schools are almost always Gothic, and the mansions and mills are never Gothic. May I ask the meaning of this; for, remember, it is peculiarly a modern phenomenon? When Gothic was invented, houses were Gothic as well as churches; and when the Italian style superseded the Gothic, churches were Italian as well as houses. If there is a Gothic spire to the cathedral of Antwerp, there is a Gothic belfry to the Hôtel de Ville at Brussels; if Inigo Jones builds an Italian Whitehall, Sir Christopher Wren builds an Italian St. Paul's. But now you live under one school of architecture, and worship under another. What do you mean by doing this? Am I to understand that you are thinking of changing your architecture back to Gothic; and that you treat your churches experimentally, because it does not matter what mistakes you make in a church? Or am I to understand that you consider Gothic a pre-eminently sacred and beautiful mode of building, which you think, like the fine frankincense, should be mixed for the tabernacle only, and reserved for your religious services? For if this be the feeling, though it may seem at first as if it were graceful and reverent, at the root of the matter, it signifies neither more nor less than that you have separated your religion from your life.

62. For consider what a wide significance this fact has; and remember that it is not you only, but all the people of England, who are behaving thus, just now.

You have all got into the habit of calling the church 'the house of God.' I have seen, over the doors of many churches, the legend actually carved, '*This* is the house of God and this is the gate of heaven.' Now, note where that legend comes from, and of what place it was first spoken. A boy leaves his father's house to go on a long journey on foot, to visit his uncle: he has to cross a wild hill-desert; just as if one of your own boys had to cross the wolds to visit an uncle at Carlisle. The second or third day your boy finds himself somewhere between Hawes and Brough, in the midst of the moors, at sunset. It is stony ground, and boggy; he cannot go one foot farther that night. Down he lies, to sleep, on Wharnside, where best he may, gathering a few of the stones together to put under his head;—so wild the place is, he cannot get anything but stones. And there, lying under the broad night, he has a dream; and he sees a ladder set up on the earth, and the top of it reaches to heaven, and the angels of God are seen ascending and descending upon it. And when he wakes out of his sleep, he says, 'How dreadful is this place; surely, this is none other than the house of God, and this is the gate of heaven.' This PLACE, observe; not this church; not this city; not this stone, even, which he puts up for a memorial—the piece of flint on which his head has lain. But this *place;* this windy slope of Wharnside; this moorland hollow, torrent-bitten, snow-blighted; this *any* place where God lets down the ladder. And how are you to know where that will be? or how are you to determine where it may be, but by being ready for it always? Do you know where the lightning is to fall next? You *do* know that, partly; you can guide the lightning; but you cannot guide the going forth of the Spirit, which is as that lightning when it shines from the east to the west.

63. But the perpetual and insolent warping of that strong verse to serve a merely ecclesiastical purpose, is only one of the thousand instances in which we sink back into gross Judaism. We call our churches 'temples.' Now, you know perfectly well they are *not* temples. They have never had, never can have, anything whatever to do with temples. They are 'synagogues'—'gathering places'—where you gather yourselves together as an assembly; and by not calling them so, you again miss the force of another

mighty text—'Thou, when thou prayest, shalt not be as the hypocrites are; for they love to pray standing in the *churches*' [we should translate it], 'that they may be seen of men. But thou, when thou prayest, enter into thy closet, and when thou hast shut thy door, pray to thy Father,'—which is, not in chancel nor in aisle, but 'in secret.'

64. Now, you feel, as I say this to you—I know you feel—as if I were trying to take away the honour of your churches. Not so; I am trying to prove to you the honour of your houses and your hills; not that the Church is not sacred—but that the whole Earth IS. I would have you feel what careless, what constant, what infectious sin there is in all modes of thought, whereby, in calling your churches only 'holy,' you call your hearths and homes 'profane'; and have separated yourselves from the heathen by casting all your household gods to the ground, instead of recognizing, in the places of their many and feeble Lares, the presence of your One and Mighty Lord and Lar.

65. 'But what has all this to do with our Exchange?' you ask me, impatiently. My dear friends, it has just everything to do with it; on these inner and great questions depend all the outer and little ones; and if you have asked me down here to speak to you, because you had before been

interested in anything I have written, you must know that all I have yet said about architecture was to show this. The book I called *The Seven Lamps* was to show that certain right states of temper and moral feeling were the magic powers by which all good architecture, without exception, had been produced. *The Stones of Venice* had, from beginning to end, no other aim than to show that the Gothic architecture of Venice had arisen out of, and indicated in all its features, a state of pure national faith, and of domestic virtue; and that its Renaissance architecture had arisen out of, and in all its features indicated, a state of concealed national infidelity, and of domestic corruption. And now, you ask me what style is best to build in; and how can I answer, knowing the meaning of the two styles, but by another question—do you mean to build as Christians or as infidels? And still more—do you mean to build as honest Christians or as honest Infidels? as thoroughly and confessedly either one or the other? You don't like to be asked such rude questions. I cannot help it; they are of much more importance than this Exchange business; and if they can be at once answered, the Exchange business settles itself in a moment. But before I press them farther, I must ask leave to explain one point clearly.

66. In all my past work, my endeavour has been to

show that good architecture is essentially religious—the production of a faithful and virtuous, not of an infidel and corrupted people. But in the course of doing this, I have had also to show that good architecture is not *ecclesiastical.* People are so apt to look upon religion as the business of the clergy, not their own, that the moment they hear of anything depending on 'religion,' they think it must also have depended on the priesthood; and I have had to take what place was to be occupied between these two errors, and fight both, often with seeming contradiction. Good architecture is the work of good and believing men; therefore, you say, at least some people say, 'Good architecture must essentially have been the work of the clergy, not of the laity.' No—a thousand times no; good architecture * has always been the work of the commonalty, *not* of the clergy. What, you say, those glorious cathedrals—the pride of Europe—did their builders not form Gothic architecture? No; they corrupted Gothic architecture. Gothic was formed in the baron's castle, and the burgher's street. It was formed by the thoughts, and hands, and powers of labouring citizens and warrior kings. By the monk it was used as an instrument for the aid of his superstition: when that superstition became a

* [And all other arts, for the most part; even of incredulous and secularly-minded commonalties.]

beautiful madness, and the best hearts of Europe vainly dreamed and pined in the cloister, and vainly raged and perished in the crusade,—through that fury of perverted faith and wasted war, the Gothic rose also to its loveliest, most fantastic, and finally, most foolish dreams; and, in those dreams, was lost.

67. I hope, now, that there is no risk of your misunderstanding me when I come to the gist of what I want to say to-night;—when I repeat, that every great national architecture has been the result and exponent of a great national religion. You can't have bits of it here, bits there—you must have it everywhere, or nowhere. It is not the monopoly of a clerical company—it is not the exponent of a theological dogma—it is not the hieroglyphic writing of an initiated priesthood; it is the manly language of a people inspired by resolute and common purpose, and rendering resolute and common fidelity to the legible laws of an undoubted God.

68. Now there have as yet been three distinct schools of European architecture. I say, European, because Asiatic and African architectures belong so entirely to other races and climates, that there is no question of them here; only, in passing, I will simply assure you that whatever is good or great in Egypt, and Syria, and India, is just good or great for the

same reasons as the buildings on our side of the Bosphorus. We Europeans, then, have had three great religions: the Greek, which was the worship of the God of Wisdom and Power; the Mediæval, which was the worship of the God of Judgment and Consolation; the Renaissance, which was the worship of the God of Pride and Beauty: these three we have had—they are past,—and now, at last, we English have got a fourth religion, and a God of our own, about which I want to ask you. But I must explain these three old ones first.

69. I repeat, first, the Greeks essentially worshipped the God of Wisdom; so that whatever contended against their religion,—to the Jews a stumbling-block,—was, to the Greeks—*Foolishness.*

The first Greek idea of deity was that expressed in the word, of which we keep the remnant in our words '*Di*-urnal' and '*Di*-vine'—the god of *Day,* Jupiter the revealer. Athena is his daughter, but especially daughter of the Intellect, springing armed from the head. We are only with the help of recent investigation beginning to penetrate the depth of meaning couched under the Athenaic symbols: but I may note rapidly, that her ægis, the mantle with the serpent fringes, in which she often, in the best statues, is represented as folding up her left hand, for better guard; and the Gorgon, on her shield, are both representative mainly of the chilling horror and sadness (turning men to stone, as it were,) of the outmost and superficial spheres of knowledge—that knowledge which separates, in bitterness, hardness, and sorrow, the heart of the full-grown man from the heart of the child. For out of imperfect knowledge spring terror, dissension, danger, and disdain; but from perfect knowledge, given by the full-revealed Athena, strength and peace, in sign of which she is crowned with the olive spray, and bears the resistless spear.

This, then, was the Greek conception of purest Deity; and every habit of life, and every form of his art developed themselves from the seeking this bright, serene, resistless wisdom; and setting himself, as a man, to do things evermore rightly and strongly;* not with any ardent affection or ultimate hope; but with a resolute and continent energy of will, as knowing that for failure there was no consolation, and for sin there was no remission. And

* [It is an error to suppose that the Greek worship, or seeking, was chiefly of Beauty. It was essentially of rightness and strength, founded on Forethought: the principal character of Greek art is not beauty, but design: and the Dorian Apollo-worship and Athenian Virgin-worship are both expressions of adoration of divine wisdom and purity. Next to these great deities, rank, in power over the national mind, Dionysius and Ceres, the givers of human strength and life: then, for heroic example, Hercules. There is no Venus-worship among the Greeks in the great times: and the Muses are essentially teachers of Truth, and of its harmonies. Compare Aratra Pentelici, § 200.]

the Greek architecture rose unerring, bright, clearly defined, and self-contained.

70. Next followed in Europe the great Christian faith, which was essentially the religion of Comfort. Its great doctrine is the remission of sins; for which cause, it happens, too often, in certain phases of Christianity, that sin and sickness themselves are partly glorified, as if, the more you had to be healed of, the more divine was the healing. The practical result of this doctrine, in art, is a continual contemplation of sin and disease, and of imaginary states of purification from them; thus we have an architecture conceived in a mingled sentiment of melancholy and aspiration, partly severe, partly luxuriant, which will bend itself to every one of our needs, and every one of our fancies, and be strong or weak with us, as we are strong or weak ourselves. It is, of all architecture, the basest, when base people build it—of all, the noblest, when built by the noble.

71. And now note that both these religions—Greek and Mediæval—perished by falsehood in their own main purpose. The Greek religion of Wisdom perished in a false philosophy—'Oppositions of science, falsely so called.' The Mediæval religion of Consolation perished in false comfort; in remission of sins given lyingly. It was the selling of absolution that ended the Mediæval faith; and I

6

can tell you more, it is the selling of absolution which, to the end of time, will mark false Christianity. Pure Christianity gives her remission of sins only by *ending* them; but false Christianity gets her remission of sins by *compounding for* them. And there are many ways of compounding for them. We English have beautiful little quiet ways of buying absolution, whether in low Church or high, far more cunning than any of Tetzel's trading.

72. Then, thirdly, there followed the religion of Pleasure, in which all Europe gave itself to luxury, ending in death. First, *bals masqués* in every saloon, and then guillotines in every square. And all these three worships issue in vast temple building. Your Greek worshipped Wisdom, and built you the Parthenon—the Virgin's temple. The Mediæval worshipped Consolation, and built you Virgin temples also—but to our Lady of Salvation. Then the Revivalist worshipped beauty, of a sort, and built you Versailles, and the Vatican. Now, lastly, will you tell me what *we* worship, and what *we* build?

73. You know we are speaking always of the real, active, continual, national worship; that by which men act, while they live; not that which they talk of, when they die. Now, we have, indeed, a nominal religion, to which we pay tithes of property and sevenths of time; but we have also a practical

and earnest religion, to which we devote nine-tenths of our property, and six-sevenths of our time. And we dispute a great deal about the nominal religion: but we are all unanimous about this practical one; of which I think you will admit that the ruling goddess may be best generally described as the 'Goddess of Getting-on,' or 'Britannia of the Market.' The Athenians had an 'Athena Agoraia,' or Athena of the Market; but she was a subordinate type of their goddess, while our Britannia Agoraia is the principal type of ours. And all your great architectural works are, of course, built to her. It is long since you built a great cathedral: and how you would laugh at me if I proposed building a cathedral on the top of one of these hills of yours, to make it an Acropolis! But your railroad mounds, vaster than the walls of Babylon; your railroad stations, vaster than the temple of Ephesus, and innumerable; your chimneys, how much more mighty and costly than cathedral spires! your harbour-piers; your warehouses; your exchanges!—all these are built to your great Goddess of 'Getting-on;' and she has formed, and will continue to form, your architecture, as long as you worship her; and it is quite vain to ask me to tell you how to build to *her;* you know far better than I.

74. There might, indeed, on some theories, be a conceivably good architecture for Exchanges—that is

to say, if there were any heroism in the fact or deed of exchange, which might be typically carved on the outside of your building. For, you know, all beautiful architecture must be adorned with sculpture or painting; and for sculpture or painting, you must have a subject. And hitherto it has been a received opinion among the nations of the world that the only right subjects for either, were *heroisms* of some sort. Even on his pots and his flagons, the Greek put a Hercules slaying lions, or an Apollo slaying serpents, or Bacchus slaying melancholy giants, and earth-born despondencies. On his temples, the Greek put contests of great warriors in founding states, or of gods with evil spirits. On his houses and temples alike, the Christian put carvings of angels conquering devils; or of hero-martyrs exchanging this world for another: subject inappropriate, I think, to our direction of exchange here. And the Master of Christians not only left his followers without any orders as to the sculpture of affairs of exchange on the outside of buildings, but gave some strong evidence of his dislike of affairs of exchange within them. And yet there might surely be a heroism in such affairs; and all commerce become a kind of selling of doves, not impious. The wonder has always been great to me, that heroism has never been supposed to be in anywise consistent with the practice of supplying people with food, or clothes; but rather with that of quartering one's self upon them for food, and stripping them of their clothes. Spoiling of armour is an heroic deed in all ages; but the selling of clothes, old, or new, has never taken any colour of magnanimity. Yet one does not see why feeding the hungry and clothing the naked should ever become base businesses, even when engaged in on a large scale. If one could contrive to attach the notion of conquest to them anyhow! so that, supposing there were anywhere an obstinate race, who refused to be comforted, one might take some pride in giving them compulsory comfort!* and, as it were, '*occupying* a country' with one's gifts, instead of one's armies? If one could only consider it as much a victory to get a barren field sown, as to get an eared field stripped; and contend who should build villages, instead of who should 'carry' them! Are not all forms of heroism conceivable in doing these serviceable deeds? You doubt who is strongest? It might be ascertained by push of spade, as well as push of sword. Who is wisest? There are witty things to be thought of in planning other business than campaigns. Who is bravest? There are always the elements to fight with, stronger than men; and nearly as merciless.

* [Quite serious, all this, though it reads like jest.]

75. The only absolutely and unapproachably heroic element in the soldier's work seems to be—that he is paid little for it—and regularly: while you traffickers, and exchangers, and others occupied in presumably benevolent business, like to be paid much for it—and by chance. I never can make out how it is that a *knight*-errant does not expect to be paid for his trouble, but a *pedlar*-errant always does;—that people are willing to take hard knocks for nothing, but never to sell ribands cheap; that they are ready to go on fervent crusades, to recover the tomb of a buried God, but never on any travels to fulfil the orders of a living one;—that they will go anywhere barefoot to preach their faith, but must be well bribed to practise it, and are perfectly ready to give the Gospel gratis, but never the loaves and fishes.*

76. If you chose to take the matter up on any such soldierly principle; to do your commerce, and your feeding of nations, for fixed salaries; and to be as particular about giving people the best food, and the best cloth, as soldiers are about giving them the best gunpowder, I could carve something for you on your exchange worth looking at. But I can only at present suggest decorating its frieze with pendant purses; and making its pillars broad at the

* [Please think over this paragraph, too briefly and antithetically put, but one of those which I am happiest in having written.]

base, for the sticking of bills. And in the innermost chambers of it there might be a statue of Britannia of the Market, who may have, perhaps advisably, a partridge for her crest, typical at once of her courage in fighting for noble ideas, and of her interest in game; and round its neck, the inscription in golden letters, 'Perdix fovit quæ non peperit.' * Then, for her spear, she might have a weaver's beam; and on her shield, instead of St. George's Cross, the Milanese boar, semi-fleeced, with the town of Gennesaret proper, in the field; and the legend, 'In the best market,'† and her corslet, of leather, folded over her heart in the shape of a purse, with thirty slits in it, for a piece of money to go in at, on each day of the month. And I doubt not but that people would come to see your exchange, and its goddess, with applause.

77. Nevertheless, I want to point out to you certain strange characters in this goddess of yours. She differs from the great Greek and Mediæval deities essentially in two things—first, as to the continuance of her presumed power; secondly, as to the extent of it.

* Jerem. xvii. 11, (best in Septuagint and Vulgate). 'As the partridge, fostering what she brought not forth, so he that getteth riches, not by right, shall leave them in the midst of his days, and at his end shall be a fool.'

† [Meaning, fully, 'We have brought our pigs to it.']

1st, as to the Continuance.

The Greek Goddess of Wisdom gave continual increase of wisdom, as the Christian Spirit of Comfort (or Comforter) continual increase of comfort. There was no question, with these, of any limit or cessation of function. But with your Agora Goddess, that is just the most important question. Getting on—but where to? Gathering together—but how much? Do you mean to gather always—never to spend? If so, I wish you joy of your goddess, for I am just as well off as you, without the trouble of worshipping her at all. But if you do not spend, somebody else will—somebody else must. And it is because of this (among many other such errors) that I have fearlessly declared your so-called science of Political Economy to be no science; because, namely, it has omitted the study of exactly the most important branch of the business—the study of *spending*. For spend you must, and as much as you make, ultimately. You gather corn:—will you bury England under a heap of grain; or will you, when you have gathered, finally eat? You gather gold:—will you make your house-roofs of it, or pave your streets with it? That is still one way of spending it. But if you keep it, that you may get more, I'll give you more; I'll give you all the gold you want—all you can imagine—if you can tell me what you'll do with it. You shall have thousands of gold pieces ;—thousands of thousands—millions—mountains, of gold : where will you keep them? Will you put an Olympus of silver upon a golden Pelion—make Ossa like a wart? Do you think the rain and dew would then come down to you, in the streams from such mountains, more blessedly than they will down the mountains which God has made for you, of moss and whinstone? But it is not gold that you want to gather! What is it? greenbacks? No; not those neither. What is it then—is it ciphers after a capital I? Cannot you practise writing ciphers, and write as many as you want? Write ciphers for an hour every morning, in a big book, and say every evening, I am worth all those noughts more than I was yesterday. Won't that do? Well, what in the name of Plutus is it you want? Not gold, not greenbacks, not ciphers after a capital I? You will have to answer, after all, 'No; we want, somehow or other, money's *worth.*' Well, what is that? Let your Goddess of Getting-on discover it, and let her learn to stay therein.

78. II. But there is yet another question to be asked respecting this Goddess of Getting-on. The first was of the continuance of her power; the second is of its extent.

Pallas and the Madonna were supposed to be all the world's Pallas, and all the world's Madonna. They could teach all men, and they could comfort all men. But, look strictly into the nature of the power of your Goddess of Getting-on; and you will find she is the Goddess—not of everybody's getting on—but only of somebody's getting on. This is a vital, or rather deathful, distinction. Examine it in your own ideal of the state of national life which this Goddess is to evoke and maintain. I asked you what it was, when I was last here; *—you have never told me. Now, shall I try to tell you?

79. Your ideal of human life then is, I think, that it should be passed in a pleasant undulating world, with iron and coal everywhere underneath it. On each pleasant bank of this world is to be a beautiful mansion, with two wings; and stables, and coach-houses; a moderately-sized park; a large garden and hot-houses; and pleasant carriage drives through the shrubberies. In this mansion are to live the favoured votaries of the Goddess; the English gentleman, with his gracious wife, and his beautiful family; he always able to have the boudoir and the jewels for the wife, and the beautiful ball dresses for the daughters, and hunters for the sons, and a shooting in the Highlands for himself. At the bottom of the

* *Two Paths*, p. 117.

bank, is to be the mill; not less than a quarter of a mile long, with one steam engine at each end, and two in the middle, and a chimney three hundred feet high. In this mill are to be in constant employment from eight hundred to a thousand workers, who never drink, never strike, always go to church on Sunday, and always express themselves in respectful language.

80. Is not that, broadly, and in the main features, the kind of thing you propose to yourselves? It is very pretty indeed, seen from above; not at all so pretty, seen from below. For, observe, while to one family this deity is indeed the Goddess of Getting-on, to a thousand families she is the Goddess of *not* Getting-on. 'Nay,' you say, 'they have all their chance.' Yes, so has every one in a lottery, but there must always be the same number of blanks. 'Ah! but in a lottery it is not skill and intelligence which take the lead, but blind chance.' What then! do you think the old practice, that 'they should take who have the power, and they should keep who can,' is less iniquitous, when the power has become power of brains instead of fist? and that, though we may not take advantage of a child's or a woman's weakness, we may of a man's foolishness? 'Nay, but finally, work must be done, and some one must be at the top, some one at the bottom.' Granted, my

friends. Work must always be, and captains of work must always be; and if you in the least remember the tone of any of my writings, you must know that they are thought unfit for this age, because they are always insisting on need of government, and speaking with scorn of liberty. But I beg you to observe that there is a wide difference between being captains or governors of work, and taking the profits of it. It does not follow, because you are general of an army, that you are to take all the treasure, or land, it wins; (if it fight for treasure or land); neither, because you are king of a nation, that you are to consume all the profits of the nation's work. Real kings, on the contrary, are known invariably by their doing quite the reverse of this,—by their taking the least possible quantity of the nation's work for themselves. There is no test of real kinghood so infallible as that. Does the crowned creature live simply, bravely, unostentatiously? probably he *is* a King. Does he cover his body with jewels, and his table with delicates? in all probability he is *not* a King. It is possible he may be, as Solomon was; but that is when the nation shares his splendour with him. Solomon made gold, not only to be in his own palace as stones, but to be in Jerusalem as stones. But, even so, for the most part, these splendid kinghoods expire in ruin, and only the true kinghoods live, which are of royal labourers governing loyal labourers; who, both leading rough lives, establish the true dynasties. Conclusively you will find that because you are king of a nation, it does not follow that you are to gather for yourself all the wealth of that nation; neither, because you are king of a small part of the nation, and lord over the means of its maintenance—over field, or mill, or mine, are you to take all the produce of that piece of the foundation of national existence for yourself.

81. You will tell me I need not preach against these things, for I cannot mend them. No, good friends, I cannot; but you can, and you will; or something else can and will. Even good things have no abiding power—and shall these evil things persist in victorious evil? All history shows, on the contrary, that to be the exact thing they never can do. Change *must* come; but it is ours to determine whether change of growth, or change of death. Shall the Parthenon be in ruins on its rock, and Bolton priory in its meadow, but these mills of yours be the consummation of the buildings of the earth, and their wheels be as the wheels of eternity? Think you that 'men may come, and men may go,' but—mills—go on for ever? Not so; out of these, better or worse shall come; and it is for you to choose which.

82. I know that none of this wrong is done

with deliberate purpose. I know, on the contrary, that you wish your workmen well; that you do much for them, and that you desire to do more for them, if you saw your way to such benevolence safely. I know that even all this wrong and misery are brought about by a warped sense of duty, each of you striving to do his best; but, unhappily, not knowing for whom this best should be done. And all our hearts have been betrayed by the plausible impiety of the modern economist, telling us that, 'To do the best for ourselves, is finally to do the best for others.' Friends, our great Master said not so; and most absolutely we shall find this world is not made so. Indeed, to do the best for others, is finally to do the best for ourselves; but it will not do to have our eyes fixed on that issue. The Pagans had got beyond that. Hear what a Pagan says of this matter; hear what were, perhaps, the last written words of Plato,—if not the last actually written (for this we cannot know), yet assuredly in fact and power his parting words—in which, endeavouring to give full crowning and harmonious close to all his thoughts, and to speak the sum of them by the imagined sentence of the Great Spirit, his strength and his heart fail him, and the words cease, broken off for ever.

83. They are at the close of the dialogue called

'Critias,' in which he describes, partly from real tradition, partly in ideal dream, the early state of Athens; and the genesis, and order, and religion, of the fabled isle of Atlantis; in which genesis he conceives the same first perfection and final degeneracy of man, which in our own Scriptural tradition is expressed by saying that the Sons of God intermarried with the daughters of men, for he supposes the earliest race to have been indeed the children of God; and to have corrupted themselves, until 'their spot was not the spot of his children.' And this, he says, was the end; that indeed 'through many generations, so long as the God's nature in them yet was full, they were submissive to the sacred laws, and carried themselves lovingly to all that had kindred with them in divineness; for their uttermost spirit was faithful and true, and in every wise great; so that, in *all meekness of wisdom, they dealt with each other*, and took all the chances of life; and despising all things except virtue, they cared little what happened day by day, and *bore lightly the burden* of gold and of possessions; for they saw that, if *only their common love and virtue increased, all these things would be increased together with them;* but to set their esteem and ardent pursuit upon material possession, would be to lose that first, and their virtue and affection together with it. And by such reasoning, and what of the divine nature remained in them, they gained all this greatness of which we have already told; but when the God's part of them faded and became extinct, being mixed again and again, and effaced by the prevalent mortality; and the human nature at last exceeded, they then became unable to endure the courses of fortune; and fell into shapelessness of life, and baseness in the sight of him who could see, having lost everything that was fairest of their honour; while to the blind hearts which could not discern the true life, tending to happiness, it seemed that they were then chiefly noble and happy, being filled with all iniquity of inordinate possession and power. Whereupon, the God of Gods, whose Kinghood is in laws, beholding a once just nation thus cast into misery, and desiring to lay such punishment upon them as might make them repent into restraining, gathered together all the gods into his dwelling place, which from heaven's centre overlooks whatever has part in creation; and having assembled them, he said'——

84. The rest is silence. Last words of the chief wisdom of the heathen, spoken of this idol of riches; this idol of yours; this golden image, high by measureless cubits, set up where your green fields of England are furnace-burnt into the likeness of the plain of Dura: this idol, forbidden to us, first of

all idols, by our own Master and faith; forbidden to us also by every human lip that has ever, in any age or people, been accounted of as able to speak according to the purposes of God. Continue to make that forbidden deity your principal one, and soon no more art, no more science, no more pleasure will be possible. Catastrophe will come; or, worse than catastrophe, slow mouldering and withering into Hades. But if you can fix some conception of a true human state of life to be striven for—life, good for all men, as for yourselves; if you can determine some honest and simple order of existence; following those trodden ways of wisdom, which are pleasantness, and seeking her quiet and withdrawn paths, which are peace;*—then, and so sanctifying wealth into 'commonwealth,' all your art, your literature, your daily labours, your domestic affection, and citizen's duty, will join and increase into one magnificent harmony. You will know then how to build, well enough; you will build with stone well, but with flesh better; temples not made with hands, but riveted of hearts; and that kind of marble, crimson-veined, is indeed eternal.

* [I imagine the Hebrew chant merely intends passionate repetition, not a distinction of this somewhat fanciful kind; yet we may profitably make it in reading the English.]

LECTURE III.

WAR.

(*Delivered at the Royal Military Academy, Woolwich*, 1865.)

85. YOUNG SOLDIERS, I do not doubt but that many of you came unwillingly to-night, and many in merely contemptuous curiosity, to hear what a writer on painting could possibly say, or would venture to say, respecting your great art of war. You may well think within yourselves, that a painter might, perhaps without immodesty, lecture younger painters upon painting, but not young lawyers upon law, nor young physicians upon medicine—least of all, it may seem to you, young warriors upon war. And, indeed, when I was asked to address you, I declined at first, and declined long; for I felt that you would not be interested in my special business, and would certainly think there was small need for me to come to teach you your's. Nay, I knew that there ought to be *no* such need, for the great veteran soldiers of England

are now men every way so thoughtful, so noble, and so good, that no other teaching than their knightly example, and their few words of grave and tried counsel, should be either necessary for you, or even, without assurance of due modesty in the offerer, endured by you.

86. But being asked, not once nor twice, I have not ventured persistently to refuse; and I will try, in very few words, to lay before you some reason why you should accept my excuse, and hear me patiently. You may imagine that your work is wholly foreign to, and separate from, mine. So far from that, all the pure and noble arts of peace are founded on war; no great art ever yet rose on earth, but among a nation of soldiers. There is no art among a shepherd people, if it remains at peace. There is no art among an agricultural people, if it remains at peace. Commerce is barely consistent with fine art; but cannot produce it. Manufacture not only is unable to produce it, but invariably destroys whatever seeds of it exist. There is no great art possible to a nation but that which is based on battle.

87. Now, though I hope you love fighting for its own sake, you must, I imagine, be surprised at my assertion that there is any such good fruit of fighting. You supposed, probably, that your office was to defend the works of peace, but certainly not to found

them: nay, the common course of war, you may have thought, was only to destroy them. And truly, I, who tell you this of the use of war, should have been the last of men to tell you so, had I trusted my own experience only. Hear why: I have given a considerable part of my life to the investigation of Venetian painting; and the result of that enquiry was my fixing upon one man as the greatest of all Venetians, and therefore, as I believed, of all painters whatsoever. I formed this faith (whether right or wrong matters at present nothing) in the supremacy of the painter Tintoret, under a roof covered with his pictures; and of those pictures, three of the noblest were then in the form of shreds of ragged canvas, mixed up with the laths of the roof, rent through by three Austrian shells. Now, it is not every lecturer who *could* tell you that he had seen three of his favourite pictures torn to rags by bomb-shells. And after such a sight, it is not every lecturer who *would* tell you that, nevertheless, war was the foundation of all great art.

88. Yet the conclusion is inevitable, from any careful comparison of the states of great historic races at different periods. Merely to show you what I mean, I will sketch for you, very briefly, the broad steps of the advance of the best art of the world. The first dawn of it is in Egypt; and the power of it

is founded on the perpetual contemplation of death, and of future judgment, by the mind of a nation of which the ruling caste were priests, and the second, soldiers. The greatest works produced by them are sculptures of their kings going out to battle, or receiving the homage of conquered armies. And you must remember also, as one of the great keys to the splendour of the Egyptian nation, that the priests were not occupied in theology only. Their theology was the basis of practical government and law; so that they were not so much priests as religious judges; the office of Samuel, among the Jews, being as nearly as possible correspondent to theirs.

89. All the rudiments of art then, and much more than the rudiments of all science, are laid first by this great warrior-nation, which held in contempt all mechanical trades, and in absolute hatred the peaceful life of shepherds. From Egypt art passes directly into Greece, where all poetry, and all painting, are nothing else than the description, praise, or dramatic representation of war, or of the exercises which prepare for it, in their connection with offices of religion. All Greek institutions had first respect to war; and their conception of it, as one necessary office of all human and divine life, is expressed simply by the images of their guiding gods. Apollo is the god of all wisdom of the intellect; he bears the

arrow and the bow, before he bears the lyre. Again, Athena is the goddess of all wisdom in conduct. Yet it is by the helmet and the shield, oftener than by the shuttle, that she is distinguished from other deities.

90. There were, however, two great differences in principle between the Greek and the Egyptian theories of policy. In Greece there was no soldier caste; every citizen was necessarily a soldier. And, again, while the Greeks rightly despised mechanical arts as much as the Egyptians, they did not make the fatal mistake of despising agricultural and pastoral life; but perfectly honoured both. These two conditions of truer thought raise them quite into the highest rank of wise manhood that has yet been reached; for all our great arts, and nearly all our great thoughts, have been borrowed or derived from them. Take away from us what they have given; and we hardly can imagine how low the modern* European would stand.

91. Now, you are to remember, in passing to the next phase of history, that though you *must* have war to produce art—you must also have much more than war; namely, an art-instinct or genius in the people; and that, though all the talent for painting

* [The *modern*, observe, because we have lost all inheritance from Florence or Venice, and are now pensioners upon the Greeks only.]

in the world won't make painters of you, unless you have a gift for fighting as well, you may have the gift for fighting, and none for painting. Now, in the next great dynasty of soldiers, the art-instinct is wholly wanting. I have not yet investigated the Roman character enough to tell you the causes of this; but I believe, paradoxical as it may seem to you, that, however truly the Roman might say of himself that he was born of Mars, and suckled by the wolf, he was nevertheless, at heart, more of a farmer than a soldier. The exercises of war were with him practical, not poetical; his poetry was in domestic life only, and the object of battle, 'pacis imponere morem.' And the arts are extinguished in his hands, and do not rise again, until, with Gothic chivalry, there comes back into the mind of Europe a passionate delight in war itself, for the sake of war. And then, with the romantic knighthood which can imagine no other noble employment,—under the fighting kings of France, England, and Spain; and under the fighting dukeships and citizenships of Italy, art is born again, and rises to her height in the great valleys of Lombardy and Tuscany, through which there flows not a single stream, from all their Alps or Apennines, that did not once run dark red from battle; and it reaches its culminating glory in the city which gave to history the most intense type of soldiership yet seen among men;—the city whose armies were led in their assault by their king,* led through it to victory by their king, and so led, though that king of theirs was blind, and in the extremity of his age.

92. And from this time forward, as peace is established or extended in Europe, the arts decline. They reach an unparalleled pitch of costliness, but lose their life, enlist themselves at last on the side of luxury and various corruption, and, among wholly tranquil nations, wither utterly away; remaining only in partial practice among races who, like the French and us, have still the minds, though we cannot all live the lives, of soldiers.

93. 'It may be so,' I can suppose that a philanthropist might exclaim. 'Perish then the arts, if they can flourish only at such a cost. What worth is there in toys of canvas and stone, if compared to the joy and peace of artless domestic life?' And the answer is—truly, in themselves, none. But as expressions of the highest state of the human spirit, their worth is infinite. As results they may be worthless, but, as signs, they are above price. For it is an assured truth that, whenever the faculties of men are at their fulness, they

* [Henry Dandolo: the king of Bohemia at Crecy is very grand, too, and in the issue, his knighthood is, to us, more memorable.]

must express themselves by art; and to say that a state is without such expression, is to say that it is sunk from its proper level of manly nature. So that, when I tell you that war is the foundation of all the arts, I mean also that it is the foundation of all the high virtues and faculties of men.

94. It was very strange to me to discover this; and very dreadful—but I saw it to be quite an undeniable fact. The common notion that peace and the virtues of civil life flourished together, I found to be wholly untenable. Peace and the *vices* of civil life only flourish together. We talk of peace and learning, and of peace and plenty, and of peace and civilisation; but I found that those were not the words which the Muse of History coupled together: that, on her lips, the words were—peace, and sensuality—peace, and selfishness—peace, and death. I found, in brief, that all great nations learned their truth of word, and strength of thought, in war; that they were nourished in war, and wasted by peace; taught by war, and deceived by peace; trained by war, and betrayed by peace;—in a word, that they were born in war, and expired in peace.

95. Yet now note carefully, in the second place, it is not *all* war of which this can be said—nor all dragon's teeth, which, sown, will start up into men.

It is not the rage of a barbarian wolf-flock, as under Genseric or Suwarrow; nor the habitual restlessness and rapine of mountaineers, as on the old borders of Scotland; nor the occasional struggle of a strong peaceful nation for its life, as in the wars of the Swiss with Austria; nor the contest of merely ambitious nations for extent of power, as in the wars of France under Napoleon, or the just terminated war in America. None of these forms of war build anything but tombs. But the creative, or foundational, war is that in which the natural restlessness and love of contest among men are disciplined, by consent, into modes of beautiful—though it may be fatal—play: in which the natural ambition and love of power of men are disciplined into the aggressive conquest of surrounding evil: and in which the natural instincts of self-defence are sanctified by the nobleness of the institutions, and purity of the households which they are appointed to defend. To such war as this all men are born; in such war as this any man may happily die; and out of such war as this have arisen throughout the extent of past ages, all the highest sanctities and virtues of humanity.

I shall therefore divide the war of which I would speak to you into three heads. War for exercise or play; war for dominion; and, war for defence.

96. I. And first, of war for exercise or play. I

speak of it primarily in this light, because, through all past history, manly war has been more an exercise than anything else, among the classes who cause and proclaim it. It is not a game to the conscript, or the pressed sailor; but neither of these are the causers of it. To the governor who determines that war shall be, and to the youths who voluntarily adopt it as their profession, it has always been a grand pastime; and chiefly pursued because they had nothing else to do. And this is true without any exception. No king whose mind was fully occupied with the development of the inner resources of his kingdom, or with any other sufficing subject of thought, ever entered into war but on compulsion. No youth who was earnestly busy with any peaceful subject of study, or set on any serviceable course of action, ever voluntarily became a soldier. Occupy him, early and wisely, in agriculture or business, in science or in literature, and he will never think of war otherwise than as a calamity.* But leave him idle; and, the more brave and active and capable he is by nature, the more he will thirst for some appointed field for action; and find, in the passion and peril of battle, the only satisfying fulfilment of his unoccupied being. And from the earliest incipient civilization until now,

* [A wholesome calamity, observe; not to be shrunk from, though not to be provoked. But see the opening of the notes on Prussia, p. 177.]

the population of the earth divides itself, when you look at it widely, into two races; one of workers, and the other of players—one tilling the ground, manufacturing, building, and otherwise providing for the necessities of life;—the other part proudly idle, and continually therefore needing recreation, in which they use the productive and laborious orders partly as their cattle, and partly as their puppets or pieces in the game of death.

97.* Now, remember, whatever virtue or goodliness there may be in this game of war, rightly played, there is none when you thus play it with a multitude of human pawns.

If you, the gentlemen of this or any other kingdom, choose to make your pastime of contest, do so, and welcome; but set not up these unhappy peasant-pieces upon the chequer of forest and field. If the wager is to be of death, lay it on your own heads, not theirs. A goodly struggle in the Olympic dust, though it be the dust of the grave, the gods will look upon, and be with you in; but they will not be with you, if you sit on the sides of the amphitheatre, whose steps are the mountains of earth, whose arena its valleys, to

* [I dislike more and more every day the declamatory forms in which what I most desired to make impressive was arranged for oral delivery; but these two paragraphs, 97 and 98, sacrifice no accuracy in their endeavour to be pompous, and are among the most importantly true passages I have ever written.]

urge your peasant millions into gladiatorial war. You also, you tender and delicate women, for whom, and by whose command, all true battle has been, and must ever be; you would perhaps shrink now, though you need not, from the thought of sitting as queens above set lists where the jousting game might be mortal. How much more, then, ought you to shrink from the thought of sitting above a theatre pit in which even a few condemned slaves were slaying each other only for your delight! And do you *not* shrink from the *fact* of sitting above a theatre pit, where,—not condemned slaves,—but the best and bravest of the poor sons of your people, slay each other,—not man to man,—as the coupled gladiators; but race to race, in duel of generations? You would tell me, perhaps, that you do not sit to see this; and it is, indeed, true that the women of Europe—those who have no heart-interest of their own at peril in the contest—draw the curtains of their boxes, and muffle the openings; so that from the pit of the circus of slaughter there may reach them only at intervals a half-heard cry, and a murmur as of the wind's sighing, when myriads of souls expire. They shut out the death-cries; and are happy, and talk wittily among themselves. That is the utter literal fact, of what our ladies do in their pleasant lives.

98. Nay, you might answer, speaking with them—

'We do not let these wars come to pass for our play, nor by our carelessness ; we cannot help them. How can any final quarrel of nations be settled otherwise than by war ?'

I cannot now delay to tell you how political quarrels might be otherwise settled. But grant that they cannot. Grant that no law of reason can be understood by nations; no law of justice submitted to by them: and that, while questions of a few acres, and of petty cash, can be determined by truth and equity, the questions which are to issue in the perishing or saving of kingdoms can be determined only by the truth of the sword, and the equity of the rifle. Grant this, and even then, judge if it will always be necessary for you to put your quarrel into the hearts of your poor, and sign your treaties with peasants' blood. You would be ashamed to do this in your own private position and power. Why should you not be ashamed also to do it in public place and power? If you quarrel with your neighbour, and the quarrel be indeterminable by law, and mortal, you and he do not send your footmen to Battersea fields to fight it out; nor do you set fire to his tenants' cottages, nor spoil their goods. You fight out your quarrel yourselves, and at your own danger, if at all. And you do not think it materially affects the arbitrement that one of you has a larger household than the other; so that, if the servants or tenants were brought into the field with their masters, the issue of the contest could not be doubtful? You either refuse the private duel, or you practise it under laws of honour, not of physical force; that so it may be, in a manner, justly concluded. Now the just or unjust conclusion of the private feud is of little moment, while the just or unjust conclusion of the public feud is of eternal moment: and yet, in this public quarrel, you take your servants' sons from their arms to fight for it, and your servants' food from their lips to support it; and the black seals on the parchment of your treaties of peace are the deserted hearth, and the fruitless field.

99. There is a ghastly ludicrousness in this, as there is mostly in these wide and universal crimes. Hear the statement of the very fact of it in the most literal words of the greatest of our English thinkers:—

'What, speaking in quite unofficial language, is the net purport and upshot of war? To my own knowledge, for example, there dwell and toil, in the British village of Dumdrudge, usually some five-hundred souls. From these, by certain "natural enemies" of the French, there are successively selected, during the French war, say thirty able-bodied men. Dumdrudge, at her own expense, has suckled and nursed them; she has, not without difficulty and sorrow, fed them up to manhood, and even trained them to crafts, so that one can weave, another build, another hammer, and the weakest can stand under thirty stone avoirdupoise. Nevertheless, amid much weeping and swearing, they are selected; all dressed in red; and shipped away, at the public charges, some two thousand miles, or say only to the south of Spain; and fed there till wanted.

'And now to that same spot in the south of Spain are thirty similar French artizans, from a French Dumdrudge, in like manner wending; till at length after infinite effort, the two parties come into actual juxtaposition; and Thirty stands fronting Thirty, each with a gun in his hand.

'Straightway the word "Fire!" is given, and they blow the souls out of one another, and in place of sixty brisk useful craftsmen, the world has sixty dead carcases, which it must bury, and anon shed tears for. Had these men any quarrel? Busy as the devil is, not the smallest! They lived far enough apart; were the entirest strangers; nay, in so wide a universe, there was even, unconsciously, by commerce, some mutual helpfulness between them. How then? Simpleton! their governors had fallen out; and instead of shooting one another, had the cunning to make these poor blockheads shoot.'—*Sartor Resartus.*

100. Positively, then, gentlemen, the game of battle must not, and shall not, ultimately be played this way. But should it be played any way? Should it, if not by your servants, be practised by yourselves? I think, yes. Both history and human instinct seem alike to say, yes. All healthy men like fighting, and like the sense of danger; all brave women like to hear of their fighting, and of their facing danger. This is a fixed instinct in the fine race of them; and I cannot help fancying that fair fight is the best play for them; and that a tournament was a better game than a steeple-chase. The time may perhaps come, in France, as well as here, for universal hurdle-races and cricketing: but I do not think universal cricket will bring out the best qualities of the nobles of either country. I use, in such question, the test which I have adopted, of the connection of war with other arts; and I reflect how, as a sculptor, I should feel, if I were asked to design a monument for a dead knight, in Westminster Abbey, with a carving of a bat at one end, and a ball at the other. It may be the remains in me only of savage Gothic prejudice; but I had rather carve it with a shield at one end, and a sword at the other. And this, observe, with no reference whatever to any story of duty done, or cause defended. Assume the knight merely to have

ridden out occasionally to fight his neighbour for exercise; assume him even a soldier of fortune, and to have gained his bread, and filled his purse, at the sword's point. Still, I feel as if it were, somehow, grander and worthier in him to have made his bread by sword play than any other play; I had rather he had made it by thrusting than by batting;—*much* rather than by betting. Much rather that he should ride war horses, than back race horses; and—I say it sternly and deliberately—much rather would I have him slay his neighbour than cheat him.

101. But remember, so far as this may be true, the game of war is only that in which the *full personal power of the human creature* is brought out in management of its weapons. And this for three reasons:—

First, the great justification of this game is that it truly, when well played, determines *who is the best man*;—who is the highest bred, the most self-denying, the most fearless, the coolest of nerve, the swiftest of eye and hand. You cannot test these qualities wholly, unless there is a clear possibility of the struggle's ending in death. It is only in the fronting of that condition that the full trial of the man, soul and body, comes out. You may go to your game of wickets, or of hurdles, or of cards, and any knavery that is in you may stay unchallenged all the while. But if the play may be ended at any moment by a lance-thrust, a man will probably make up his accounts a little before he enters it. Whatever is rotten and evil in him will weaken his hand more in holding a sword-hilt than in balancing a billiard-cue; and on the whole, the habit of living lightly hearted, in daily presence of death, always has had, and must have, power both in the making and testing of honest men. But for the final testing, observe, you must make the issue of battle strictly dependent on fineness of frame, and firmness of hand. You must not make it the question, which of the combatants has the longest gun, or which has got behind the biggest tree, or which has the wind in his face, or which has gunpowder made by the best chemists, or iron smelted with the best coal, or the angriest mob at his back. Decide your battle, whether of nations or individuals, on *those* terms;—and you have only multiplied confusion, and added slaughter to iniquity. But decide your battle by pure trial which has the strongest arm, and steadiest heart,—and you have gone far to decide a great many matters besides, and to decide them rightly.*

102. And the other reasons for this mode of

* Compare *Fors Clavigera*, Letter XIV. p. 9.

decision of cause, are the diminution both of the material destructiveness, or cost, and of the physical distress of war. For you must not think that in speaking to you in this (as you may imagine) fantastic praise of battle, I have overlooked the conditions weighing against me. I pray all of you, who have not read, to read with the most earnest attention, Mr. Helps' two essays, on War, and Government, in the first volume of the last series of *Friends in Council.* Everything that can be urged against war is there simply, exhaustively, and most graphically stated. And all, there urged, is true. But the two great counts of evil alleged against war by that most thoughtful writer, hold only against modern war. If you have to take away masses of men from all industrial employment,—to feed them by the labour of others,—to provide them with destructive machines, varied daily in national rivalship of inventive cost; if you have to ravage the country which you attack,—to destroy, for a score of future years, its roads, its woods, its cities, and its harbours;—and if, finally, having brought masses of men, counted by hundreds of thousands, face to face, you tear those masses to pieces with jagged shot, and leave the living creatures, countlessly beyond all help of surgery, to starve and parch, through days of torture, down into clots of clay—what book of accounts shall record the cost of your work;—What book of judgment sentence the guilt of it?

103. That, I say, is *modern* war,—scientific war,—chemical and mechanic war,—how much worse than the savage's poisoned arrow! And yet you will tell me, perhaps, that any other war than this is impossible now. It may be so; the progress of science cannot, perhaps, be otherwise registered than by new facilities of destruction; and the brotherly love of our enlarging Christianity be only proved by multiplication of murder. Yet hear, for a moment, what war was, in Pagan and ignorant days;—what war might yet be, if we could extinguish our science in darkness, and join the heathen's practice to the Christian's creed. I read you this from a book which probably most of you know well, and all ought to know—Muller's 'Dorians;'*—but I have put the points I wish you to remember in closer connection than in his text.

104. 'The chief characteristic of the warriors of Sparta was great composure and a subdued strength; the violence (λύσσα) of Aristodemus and Isadas being considered as deserving rather of blame than praise; and these qualities in general distinguished the Greeks from the northern Barbarians, whose boldness always consisted in noise and tumult. For

* Vol. ii. Chap. 12, § 9.

the same reason the Spartans *sacrificed to the Muses* before an action; these goddesses being expected to produce regularity and order in battle; as they *sacrificed on the same occasion in Crete to the god of love,* as the confirmer of mutual esteem and shame. Every man put on a crown, when the band of flute-players gave the signal for attack; all the shields of the line glittered with their high polish, and mingled their splendour with the dark red of the purple mantles, which were meant both to adorn the combatant, and to conceal the blood of the wounded; to fall well and decorously being an incentive the more to the most heroic valour. The conduct of the Spartans in battle denotes a high and noble disposition, which rejected all the extremes of brutal rage. The pursuit of the enemy ceased when the victory was completed; and after the signal for retreat had been given, all hostilities ceased. The spoiling of arms, at least during the battle, was also interdicted; and the consecration of the spoils of slain enemies to the gods, as, in general, all rejoicings for victory, were considered as ill-omened.'

105. Such was the war of the greatest soldiers who prayed to heathen gods. What Christian war is, preached by Christian ministers, let any one tell you, who saw the sacred crowning, and heard the sacred

flute-playing, and was inspired and sanctified by the divinely-measured and musical language, of any North American regiment preparing for its charge. And what is the relative cost of life in pagan and Christian wars, let this one fact tell you:—the Spartans won the decisive battle of Corinth with the loss of eight men; the victors at indecisive Gettysburg confess to the loss of 30,000.

106. II. I pass now to our second order of war, the commonest among men, that undertaken in desire of dominion. And let me ask you to think for a few moments what the real meaning of this desire of dominion is—first in the minds of kings—then in that of nations.

Now, mind you this first,—that I speak either about kings, or masses of men, with a fixed conviction that human nature is a noble and beautiful thing; not a foul nor a base thing. All the sin of men I esteem as their disease, not their nature; as a folly which may be prevented, not a necessity which must be accepted. And my wonder, even when things are at their worst, is always at the height which this human nature can attain. Thinking it high, I find it always a higher thing than I thought it; while those who think it low, find it, and will find it, always, lower than they thought it: the fact being, that it is infinite, and capable of infinite height and infinite fall; but the nature of it—and here is the faith which I would have you hold with me—the *nature* of it is in the nobleness, not in the catastrophe.

107. Take the faith in its utmost terms. When the captain of the *London* shook hands with his mate, saying 'God speed you! I will go down with my passengers,' *that* I believe to be 'human nature.' He does not do it from any religious motive,—from any hope of reward, or any fear of punishment; he does it because he is a man. But when a mother, living among the fair fields of merry England, gives her two-year-old child to be suffocated under a mattress in her inner room, while the said mother waits and talks outside; *that* I believe to be *not* human nature. You have the two extremes there, shortly. And you, men, and mothers, who are here face to face with me to-night, I call upon you to say which of these is human, and which inhuman,—which 'natural' and which 'unnatural.' Choose your creed at once, I beseech you:—choose it with unshaken choice,—choose it for ever. Will you take, for foundation of act and hope, the faith that this man was such as God made him, or that this woman was such as God made her? Which of them has failed from their nature,—from their present, possible, actual nature;—not their nature of long ago, but their nature of now? Which has betrayed it—falsified

it? Did the guardian who died in his trust, die inhumanly, and as a fool; and did the murderess of her child fulfil the law of her being? Choose, I say; infinitude of choices hang upon this. You have had false prophets among you,—for centuries you have had them,—solemnly warned against them though you were; false prophets, who have told you that all men are nothing but fiends or wolves, half beast, half devil. Believe that, and indeed you may sink to that. But refuse that, and have faith that God 'made you upright,' though *you* have sought out many inventions; so, you will strive daily to become more what your Maker meant and means you to be, and daily gives you also the power to be,—and you will cling more and more to the nobleness and virtue that is in you, saying, 'My righteousness I hold fast, and will not let it go.'

108. I have put this to you as a choice, as if you might hold either of these creeds you liked best. But there is in reality no choice for you; the facts being quite easily ascertainable. You have no business to *think* about this matter, or to choose in it. The broad fact is, that a human creature of the highest race, and most perfect as a human thing, is invariably both kind and true; and that as you lower the race, you get cruelty and falseness, as you get deformity: and this so steadily and assuredly, that

the two great words which, in their first use, meant only perfection of race, have come, by consequence of the invariable connection of virtue with the fine human nature, both to signify benevolence of disposition. The word 'generous,' and the word 'gentle,' both, in their origin, meant only 'of pure race,' but because charity and tenderness are inseparable from this purity of blood, the words which once stood only for pride, now stand as synonyms for virtue.

109. Now, this being the true power of our inherent humanity, and seeing that all the aim of education should be to develope this;—and seeing also what magnificent self-sacrifice the higher classes of men are capable of, for any cause that they understand or feel,—it is wholly inconceivable to me how well-educated princes, who ought to be of all gentlemen the gentlest, and of all nobles the most generous, and whose title of royalty means only their function of doing every man '*right*'—how these, I say, throughout history, should so rarely pronounce themselves on the side of the poor and of justice, but continually maintain themselves and their own interests by oppression of the poor, and by wresting of justice; and how this should be accepted as so natural, that the word loyalty, which means faithfulness to law, is used as if it were only the duty of a people to be loyal to their king, and not the duty

of a king to be infinitely more loyal to his people. How comes it to pass that a captain will die with his passengers, and lean over the gunwale to give the parting boat its course; but that a king will not usually die with, much less *for*, his passengers—thinks it rather incumbent on his passengers, in any number, to die for *him?*

110. Think, I beseech you, of the wonder of this. The sea captain, not captain by divine right, but only by company's appointment;—not a man of royal descent, but only a plebeian who can steer;—not with the eyes of the world upon him, but with feeble chance, depending on one poor boat, of his name being ever heard above the wash of the fatal waves; not with the cause of a nation resting on his act, but helpless to save so much as a child from among the lost crowd with whom he resolves to be lost,—yet goes down quietly to his grave, rather than break his faith to these few emigrants. But your captain by divine right,—your captain with the hues of a hundred shields of kings upon his breast,—your captain whose every deed, brave or base, will be illuminated or branded for ever before unescapable eyes of men,—your captain whose every thought and act are beneficent, or fatal, from sunrising to setting, blessing as the sunshine, or shadowing as the night,—this captain, as you find him in history, for the most part thinks

only how he may tax his passengers, and sit at most ease in his state cabin!

111. For observe, if there had been indeed in the hearts of the rulers of great multitudes of men any such conception of work for the good of those under their command, as there is in the good and thoughtful masters of any small company of men, not only wars for the sake of mere increase of power, could never take place, but our idea of power itself would be entirely altered. Do you suppose that to think and act even for a million of men, to hear their complaints, watch their weaknesses, restrain their vices, make laws for them, lead them, day by day, to purer life, is not enough for one man's work? If any of us were absolute lord only of a district of a hundred miles square, and were resolved on doing our utmost for it; making it feed as large a number of people as possible; making every clod productive, and every rock defensive, and every human being happy; should we not have enough on our hands, think you?

112. But if the ruler has any other aim than this; if, careless of the result of his interference, he desire only the authority to interfere; and, regardless of what is ill-done or well-done, cares only that it shall be done at his bidding;—if he would rather do two hundred miles' space of mischief, than one hundred

miles' space of good, of course he will try to add to his territory; and to add illimitably. But does he add to his power? Do you call it power in a child, if he is allowed to play with the wheels and bands of some vast engine, pleased with their murmur and whirl, till his unwise touch, wandering where it ought not, scatters beam and wheel into ruin? Yet what machine is so vast, so incognizable, as the working of the mind of a nation; what child's touch so wanton, as the word of a selfish king? And yet, how long have we allowed the historian to speak of the extent of the calamity a man causes, as a just ground for his pride; and to extol him as the greatest prince, who is only the centre of the widest error. Follow out this thought by yourselves; and you will find that all power, properly so called, is wise and benevolent. There may be capacity in a drifting fire-ship to destroy a fleet; there may be venom enough in a dead body to infect a nation:—but which of you, the most ambitious, would desire a drifting kinghood, robed in consuming fire, or a poison-dipped sceptre whose touch was mortal? There is no true potency, remember, but that of help; nor true ambition, but ambition to save.

113. And then, observe farther, this true power, the power of saving, depends neither on multitude of men, nor on extent of territory. We are continually

assuming that nations become strong according to their numbers. They indeed become so, if those numbers can be made of one mind; but how are you sure you can stay them in one mind, and keep them from having north and south minds? Grant them unanimous, how know you they will be unanimous in right? If they are unanimous in wrong, the more they are, essentially the weaker they are. Or, suppose that they can neither be of one mind, nor of two minds, but can only be of *no* mind? Suppose they are a mere helpless mob; tottering into precipitant catastrophe, like a waggon-load of stones when the wheel comes off. Dangerous enough for their neighbours, certainly, but not 'powerful.'

114. Neither does strength depend on extent of territory, any more than upon number of population. Take up your maps when you go home this evening, —put the cluster of British Isles beside the mass of South America; and then consider whether any race of men need care how much ground they stand upon. The strength is in the men, and in their unity and virtue, not in their standing room: a little group of wise hearts is better than a wilderness full of fools; and only that nation gains true territory, which gains itself.

115. And now for the brief practical outcome of all this. Remember, no government is ultimately

strong, but in proportion to its kindness and justice; and that a nation does not strengthen, by merely multiplying and diffusing itself. We have not strengthened as yet, by multiplying into America. Nay, even when it has not to encounter the separating conditions of emigration, a nation need not boast itself of multiplying on its own ground, if it multiplies only as flies or locusts do, with the god of flies for its god. It multiplies its strength only by increasing as one great family, in perfect fellowship and brotherhood. And lastly, it does not strengthen itself by seizing dominion over races whom it cannot benefit. Austria is not strengthened, but weakened, by her grasp of Lombardy; and whatever apparent increase of majesty and of wealth may have accrued to us from the possession of India, whether these prove to us ultimately power or weakness, depends wholly on the degree in which our influence on the native race shall be benevolent and exalting.

116. But, as it is at their own peril that any race extends their dominion in mere desire of power, so it is at their own still greater peril that they refuse to undertake aggressive war, according to their force, whenever they are assured that their authority would be helpful and protective. Nor need you listen to any sophistical objection of the impossibility of knowing when a people's help is

needed, or when not. Make your national conscience clean, and your national eyes will soon be clear. No man who is truly ready to take part in a noble quarrel will ever stand long in doubt by whom, or in what cause, his aid is needed. I hold it my duty to make no political statement of any special bearing in this presence; but I tell you broadly and boldly, that, within these last ten years, we English have, as a knightly nation, lost our spurs: we have fought where we should not have fought, for gain; and we have been passive where we should not have been passive, for fear. I tell you that the principle of non-intervention, as now preached among us, is as selfish and cruel as the worst frenzy of conquest, and differs from it only by being, not only malignant, but dastardly.

117. I know, however, that my opinions on this subject differ too widely from those ordinarily held, to be any farther intruded upon you; and therefore I pass lastly to examine the conditions of the third kind of noble war;—war waged simply for defence of the country in which we were born, and for the maintenance and execution of her laws, by whomsoever threatened or defied. It is to this duty that I suppose most men entering the army consider themselves in reality to be bound, and I want you now to reflect what the laws of mere defence

are; and what the soldier's duty, as now understood, or supposed to be understood. You have solemnly devoted yourselves to be English soldiers, for the guardianship of England. I want you to feel what this vow of yours indeed means, or is gradually coming to mean.

118. You take it upon you, first, while you are sentimental schoolboys; you go into your military convent, or barracks, just as a girl goes into her convent while she is a sentimental schoolgirl; neither of you then know what you are about, though both the good soldiers and good nuns make the best of it afterwards. You don't understand perhaps why I call you 'sentimental' schoolboys, when you go into the army? Because, on the whole, it is the love of adventure, of excitement, of fine dress and of the pride of fame, all which are sentimental motives, which chiefly make a boy like going into the Guards better than into a counting-house. You fancy, perhaps, that there is a severe sense of duty mixed with these peacocky motives? And in the best of you there is; but do not think that it is principal. If you cared to do your duty to your country in a prosaic and unsentimental way, depend upon it, there is now truer duty to be done in raising harvests, than in burning them; more in building houses, than in shelling them—more in

winning money by your own work, wherewith to help men, than in taxing other people's work, for money wherewith to slay men;—more duty finally, in honest and unselfish living than in honest and unselfish dying, though that seems to your boys' eyes the bravest. So far, then, as for your own honour, and the honour of your families, you choose brave death in a red coat before brave life in a black one, you are sentimental; and now see what this passionate vow of yours comes to. For a little while you ride, and you hunt tigers or savages, you shoot, and are shot; you are happy, and proud, always, and honoured and wept if you die; and you are satisfied with your life, and with the end of it; believing, on the whole, that good rather than harm of it comes to others, and much pleasure to you.

119. But as the sense of duty enters into your forming minds, the vow takes another aspect. You find that you have put yourselves into the hand of your country as a weapon. You have vowed to strike, when she bids you, and to stay scabbarded when she bids you; all that you need answer for is, that you fail not in her grasp. And there is goodness in this, and greatness, if you can trust the hand and heart of the Britomart who has braced you to her side, and are assured that when she leaves you sheathed in darkness, there is no need for your flash

to the sun. But remember, good and noble as this state may be, it is a state of slavery. There are different kinds of slaves and different masters. Some slaves are scourged to their work by whips, others are scourged to it by restlessness or ambition. It does not matter what the whip is; it is none the less a whip, because you have cut thongs for it out of your own souls: the fact, so far, of slavery, is in being driven to your work without thought, at another's bidding. Again, some slaves are bought with money, and others with praise. It matters not what the purchase-money is. The distinguishing sign of slavery is to have a price, and be bought for it. Again, it matters not what kind of work you are set on; some slaves are set to forced diggings, others to forced marches; some dig furrows, others field-works, and others graves. Some press the juice of reeds, and some the juice of vines, and some the blood of men. The fact of the captivity is the same, whatever work we are set upon, though the fruits of the toil may be different.

120. But, remember, in thus vowing ourselves to be the slaves of any master, it ought to be some subject of forethought with us, what work he is likely to put us upon. You may think that the whole duty of a soldier is to be passive, that it is the country you have left behind who is to command, and you have

only to obey. But are you sure that you have left *all* your country behind, or that the part of it you have so left is indeed the best part of it? Suppose—and, remember, it is quite conceivable—that you yourselves are indeed the best part of England; that you, who have become the slaves, ought to have been the masters; and that those who are the masters, ought to have been the slaves! If it is a noble and whole-hearted England, whose bidding you are bound to do, it is well; but if you are yourselves the best of her heart, and the England you have left be but a half-hearted England, how say you of your obedience? You were too proud to become shop-keepers: are you satisfied, then, to become the servants of shopkeepers? You were too proud to become merchants or farmers yourselves: will you have merchants or farmers, then, for your field-marshals? You had no gifts of special grace for Exeter Hall: will you have some gifted person thereat for your commander-in-chief, to judge of your work, and reward it? You imagine yourselves to be the army of England: how if you should find yourselves, at last, only the police of her manufacturing towns, and the beadles of her Little Bethels?

121. It is not so yet, nor will be so, I trust, for ever; but what I want you to see, and to be assured of, is, that the ideal of soldiership is not mere

passive obedience and bravery; that, so far from this, no country is in a healthy state which has separated, even in a small degree, her civil from her military power. All states of the world, however great, fall at once when they use mercenary armies; and although it is a less instant form of error (because involving no national taint of cowardice), it is yet an error no less ultimately fatal—it is the error especially of modern times, of which we cannot yet know all the calamitous consequences,—to take away the best blood and strength of the nation, all the soul-substance of it that is brave, and careless of reward, and scornful of pain, and faithful in trust; and to cast that into steel, and make a mere sword of it; taking away its voice and will; but to keep the worst part of the nation—whatever is cowardly, avaricious, sensual, and faithless—and to give to this the voice, to this the authority, to this the chief privilege, where there is least capacity, of thought.

122. The fulfilment of your vow for the defence of England will by no means consist in carrying out such a system. You are not true soldiers, if you only mean to stand at a shop-door, to protect shop-boys who are cheating inside. A soldier's vow to his country is that he will die for the guardianship of her domestic virtue, of her righteous laws, and of her any-way challenged or endangered honour. A state

without virtue, without laws, and without honour, he is bound *not* to defend; nay, bound to redress by his own right hand that which he sees to be base in her.

123. So sternly is this the law of Nature and life, that a nation once utterly corrupt can only be redeemed by a military despotism—never by talking, nor by its free effort. And the health of any state consists simply in this; that in it, those who are wisest shall also be strongest; its rulers should be also its soldiers; or, rather, by force of intellect more than of sword, its soldiers also its rulers. Whatever the hold which the aristocracy of England has on the heart of England, in that they are still always in front of her battles, this hold will not be enough, unless they are also in front of her thoughts. And truly her thoughts need good captain's leading now, if ever! Do you know what, by this beautiful division of labour (her brave men fighting, and her cowards thinking), she has come at last to think? Here is a paper in my hand,* a good one too, and an honest

* [I do not care to refer to the journal quoted, because the article was unworthy of its general tone, though in order to enable the audience to verify the quoted sentence, I left the number containing it on the table, when I gave this lecture. But a saying of Baron Liebig's, quoted at the head of a leader on the same subject in the *Daily Telegraph* of January 11, 1866, summarily digests and presents the maximum folly of modern thought in this respect. 'Civilization,' says the Baron, 'is the economy of power, and English power is coal.'

one; quite representative of the best common public thought of England at this moment; and it is holding forth in one of its leaders upon our 'social welfare,'—upon our 'vivid life'—upon the 'political supremacy of Great Britain.' And what do you think all these are owing to? To what our English sires have done for us, and taught us, age after age? No: not to that. To our honesty of heart, or coolness of head, or steadiness of will? No: not to these. To our thinkers, or our statesmen, or our poets, or our captains, or our martyrs, or the patient labour of our poor? No: not to these; or at least not to these in any chief measure. Nay, says the journal, 'more than any agency, it is the cheapness and abundance of our coal which have made us what we are.' If it be so, then 'ashes to ashes' be our epitaph! and the sooner the better.

124. Gentlemen of England, if ever you would have your country breathe the pure breath of heaven again, and receive again a soul into her body, instead of rotting into a carcase, blown up in the belly with carbonic acid (and great *that* way), you must think, and feel, for your England, as well as fight for her:

Not altogether so, my chemical friend. Civilization is the making of civil persons, which is a kind of distillation of which alembics are incapable, and does not at all imply the turning of a small company of gentlemen into a large company of ironmongers. And English power (what little of it may be left) is by no means coal, but, indeed, of that which, 'when the whole world turns to coal, then chiefly lives.']

you must teach her that all the true greatness she ever had, she won while her fields were green and her faces ruddy; and that greatness is still possible for Englishmen, even though the ground be not hollow under their feet, nor the sky black over their heads.

125. And bear with me, you soldier youths, who are thus in all ways the hope of your country, or must be, if she have any hope;—if I urge you with rude earnestness to remember that your fitness for all future trust depends upon what you are now. No good soldier in his old age was ever careless or indolent in his youth. Many a giddy and thoughtless boy has become a good bishop, or a good lawyer, or a good merchant; but no such an one ever became a good general. I challenge you, in all history, to find a record of a good soldier who was not grave and earnest in his youth. And, in general, I have no patience with people who talk of 'the thoughtlessness of youth' indulgently. I had infinitely rather hear of thoughtless old age, and the indulgence due to *that*. When a man has done his work, and nothing can any way be materially altered in his fate, let him forget his toil, and jest with his fate, if he will; but what excuse can you find for wilfulness of thought, at the very time when every crisis of future fortune hangs on your decisions? A youth thoughtless!

when all the happiness of his home for ever depends on the chances, or the passions, of an hour! A youth thoughtless! when the career of all his days depends on the opportunity of a moment! A youth thoughtless! when his every act is as a torch to the laid train of future conduct, and every imagination a fountain of life or death! Be thoughtless in *any* after years, rather than now—though, indeed, there is only one place where a man may be nobly thoughtless,—his death-bed. No thinking should ever be left to be done *there*.

126. Having, then, resolved that you will not waste recklessly, but earnestly use, these early days of yours, remember that all the duties of her children to England may be summed in two words—industry, and honour. I say, first, industry, for it is in this that soldier youth are especially tempted to fail. Yet, surely, there is no reason, because your life may possibly or probably be shorter than other men's, that you should therefore waste more recklessly the portion of it that is granted you; neither do the duties of your profession, which require you to keep your bodies strong, in any wise involve the keeping of your minds weak. So far from that, the experience, the hardship, and the activity of a soldier's life render his powers of thought more accurate than those of other men; and while, for others, all knowledge is often

little more than a means of amusement, there is no form of science which a soldier may not at some time or other find bearing on business of life and death. A young mathematician may be excused for languor in studying curves to be described only with a pencil; but not in tracing those which are to be described with a rocket. Your knowledge of a wholesome herb may involve the feeding of an army; and acquaintance with an obscure point of geography, the success of a campaign. Never waste an instant's time, therefore: the sin of idleness is a thousand-fold greater in you than in other youths; for the fates of those who will one day be under your command hang upon your knowledge; lost moments now will be lost lives then, and every instant which you carelessly take for play, you buy with blood.

127. But there is one way of wasting time, of all the vilest, because it wastes, not time only, but the interest and energy of your minds. Of all the ungentlemanly habits into which you can fall, the vilest is betting, or interesting yourselves in the issues of betting. It unites nearly every condition of folly and vice; you concentrate your interest upon a matter of chance, instead of upon a subject of true knowledge; and you back opinions which you have no grounds for forming, merely because they are your own. All the insolence of egotism is in this; and so

far as the love of excitement is complicated with the hope of winning money, you turn yourselves into the basest sort of tradesmen—those who live by speculation. Were there no other ground for industry, this would be a sufficient one; that it protected you from the temptation to so scandalous a vice. Work faithfully, and you will put yourselves in possession of a glorious and enlarging happiness; not such as can be won by the speed of a horse, or marred by the obliquity of a ball.

128. First, then, by industry you must fulfil your vow to your country; but all industry and earnestness will be useless unless they are consecrated by your resolution to be in all things men of honour; not honour in the common sense only, but in the highest. Rest on the force of the two main words in the great verse, '*integer* vitæ, scelerisque *purus*.' You have vowed your life to England; give it her wholly;—a bright, stainless, perfect life—a knightly life. Because you have to fight with machines instead of lances, there may be a necessity for more ghastly danger, but there is none for less worthiness of character, than in olden time. You may be true knights yet, though perhaps not *equites;* you may have to call yourselves 'canonry' instead of 'chivalry,' but that is no reason why you should not call yourselves true men. So the first thing you have to see to

in becoming soldiers is that you make yourselves wholly true. Courage is a mere matter of course among any ordinarily well-born youths; but neither truth nor gentleness is matter of course. You must bind them like shields about your necks; you must write them on the tables of your hearts. Though it be not exacted of you, yet exact it of yourselves, this vow of stainless truth. Your hearts are, if you leave them unstirred, as tombs in which a god lies buried. Vow yourselves crusaders to redeem that sacred sepulchre. And remember, before all things—for no other memory will be so protective of you—that the highest law of this knightly truth is that under which it is vowed to women. Whomsoever else you deceive, whomsoever you injure, whomsoever you leave unaided, you must not deceive, nor injure, nor leave unaided, according to your power, any woman, of whatever rank. Believe me, every virtue of the higher phases of manly character begins in this;—in truth and modesty before the face of all maidens; in truth and pity, or truth and reverence, to all womanhood.

129. And now let me turn for a moment to you,—wives and maidens, who are the souls of soldiers; to you,—mothers, who have devoted your children to the great hierarchy of war. Let me ask you to consider what part you have to take for the aid of those

who love you ; for if you fail in your part they cannot fulfil theirs ; such absolute helpmates you are that no man can stand without that help, nor labour in his own strength.

I know your hearts, and that the truth of them never fails when an hour of trial comes which you recognize for such. But you know not when the hour of trial first finds you, nor when it verily finds you. You imagine that you are only called upon to wait and to suffer ; to surrender and to mourn. You know that you must not weaken the hearts of your husbands and lovers, even by the one fear of which those hearts are capable,—the fear of parting from you, or of causing you grief. Through weary years of separation ; through fearful expectancies of unknown fate ; through the tenfold bitterness of the sorrow which might so easily have been joy, and the tenfold yearning for glorious life struck down in its prime ;—through all these agonies you fail not, and never will fail. But your trial is not in these. To be heroic in danger is little ;—you are Englishwomen. To be heroic in change and sway of fortune is little ; —for do you not love ? To be patient through the great chasm and pause of loss is little ;—for do you not still love in heaven ? But to be heroic in happiness ; to bear yourselves gravely and righteously in the dazzling of the sunshine of morning ; not to forget the God in whom you trust, when He gives you most; not to fail those who trust you, when they seem to need you least; this is the difficult fortitude. It is not in the pining of absence, not in the peril of battle, not in the wasting of sickness, that your prayer should be most passionate, or your guardianship most tender. Pray, mothers and maidens, for your young soldiers in the bloom of their pride; pray for them, while the only dangers round them are in their own wayward wills; watch you, and pray, when they have to face, not death, but temptation. But it is this fortitude also for which there is the crowning reward. Believe me, the whole course and character of your lovers' lives is in your hands: what you would have them be, they shall be, if you not only desire to have them so, but deserve to have them so; for they are but mirrors in which you will see yourselves imaged. If you are frivolous, they will be so also; if you have no understanding of the scope of their duty, they also will forget it; they will listen,—they *can* listen,—to no other interpretation of it than that uttered from your lips. Bid them be brave;—they will be brave for you: bid them be cowards:—and how noble soever they be, they will quail for you. Bid them be wise, and they will be wise for you; mock at their counsel, they will be fools for you: such and so absolute is your rule over them. You fancy, perhaps, as you have been told so often, that a wife's rule should only be over her husband's house, not over his mind. Ah, no! the true rule is just the reverse of that; a true wife, in her husband's house, is his servant; it is in his heart that she is queen. Whatever of best he can conceive, it is her part to be; whatever of highest he can hope, it is hers to promise; all that is dark in him she must purge into purity; all that is failing in him she must strengthen into truth; from her, through all the world's clamour, he must win his praise; in her, through all the world's warfare, he must find his peace.

130. And, now, but one word more. You may wonder, perhaps, that I have spoken all this night in praise of war. Yet, truly, if it might be, I for one, would fain join in the cadence of hammer-strokes that should beat swords into ploughshares: and that this cannot be, is not the fault of us men. It is *your* fault. Wholly yours. Only by your command, or by your permission, can any contest take place among us. And the real, final, reason for all the poverty, misery, and rage of battle, throughout Europe, is simply that you women, however good, however religious, however self-sacrificing for those whom you love, are too selfish and too thoughtless to take pains for any creature out of your own immediate circles. You fancy that you are sorry for the pain of others.

Now I just tell you this, that if the usual course of war, instead of unroofing peasants' houses, and ravaging peasants' fields, merely broke the china upon your own drawing-room tables, no war in civilized countries would last a week. I tell you more, that at whatever moment you chose to put a period to war, you could do it with less trouble than you take any day to go out to dinner. You know, or at least you might know if you would think, that every battle you hear of has made many widows and orphans. We have, none of us, heart enough truly to mourn with these. But at least we might put on the outer symbols of mourning with them. Let but every Christian lady who has conscience toward God, vow that she will mourn, at least outwardly, for His killed creatures. Your praying is useless, and your church-going mere mockery of God, if you have not plain obedience in you enough for this. Let every lady in the upper classes of civilized Europe simply vow that, while any cruel war proceeds, she will wear *black*;—a mute's black,—with no jewel, no ornament, no excuse for, or evasion into, prettiness—I tell you again, no war would last a week.

131. And, lastly. You women of England are all now shrieking with one voice,—you and your clergymen together,—because you hear of your Bibles being attacked. If you choose to obey your Bibles,

you will never care who attacks them. It is just because you never fulfil a single downright precept of the Book, that you are so careful for its credit: and just because you don't care to obey its whole words, that you are so particular about the letters of them. The Bible tells you to dress plainly,—and you are mad for finery; the Bible tells you to have pity on the poor,—and you crush them under your carriage-wheels; the Bible tells you to do judgment and justice,—and you do not know, nor care to know, so much as what the Bible word 'justice' means. Do but learn so much of God's truth as that comes to; know what He means when He tells you to be just; and teach your sons, that their bravery is but a fool's boast, and their deeds but a firebrand's tossing, unless they are indeed Just men, and Perfect in the Fear of God:—and you will soon have no more war, unless it be indeed such as is willed by Him, of whom, though Prince of Peace, it is also written, 'In Righteousness He doth judge, and make war.'

LECTURE IV.

THE FUTURE OF ENGLAND.

(*Delivered at the R.A. Institution, Woolwich, December* 14, 1869.)

132. I WOULD fain have left to the frank expression of the moment, but fear I could not have found clear words—I cannot easily find them, even deliberately,—to tell you how glad I am, and yet how ashamed, to accept your permission to speak to you. Ashamed of appearing to think that I can tell you any truth which you have not more deeply felt than I; but glad in the thought that my less experience, and way of life sheltered from the trials, and free from the responsibilities of yours, may have left me with something of a child's power of help to you; a sureness of hope, which may perhaps be the one thing that *can* be helpful to men who have done too much not to have often failed in doing all that they desired. And indeed, even the most hopeful of us, cannot but now be in

many things apprehensive. For this at least we all know too well, that we are on the eve of a great political crisis, if not of political change. That a struggle is approaching between the newly-risen power of democracy and the apparently departing power of feudalism; and another struggle, no less imminent, and far more dangerous, between wealth and pauperism. These two quarrels are constantly thought of as the same. They are being fought together, and an apparently common interest unites for the most part the millionaire with the noble, in resistance to a multitude, crying, part of it for bread and part of it for liberty.

133. And yet no two quarrels can be more distinct. Riches—so far from being necessary to noblesse—are adverse to it. So utterly adverse, that the first character of all the Nobilities which have founded great dynasties in the world is to be poor;—often poor by oath—always poor by generosity. And of every true knight in the chivalric ages, the first thing history tells you is, that he never kept treasure for himself.

134. Thus the causes of wealth and noblesse are not the same; but opposite. On the other hand, the causes of anarchy and of the poor are not the same, but opposite. Side by side, in the same rank, are now indeed set the pride that revolts

against authority, and the misery that appeals against avarice. But, so far from being a common cause, all anarchy is the forerunner of poverty, and all prosperity begins in obedience. So that, thus, it has become impossible to give due support to the cause of order, without seeming to countenance injury; and impossible to plead justly the claims of sorrow, without seeming to plead also for those of license.

Let me try, then, to put in very brief terms, the real plan of this various quarrel, and the truth of the cause on each side. Let us face that full truth, whatever it may be, and decide what part, according to our power, we should take in the quarrel.

135. First. For eleven hundred years, all but five, since Charlemagne set on his head the Lombard crown, the body of European people have submitted patiently to be governed; generally by kings—always by single leaders of some kind. But for the last fifty years they have begun to suspect, and of late they have many of them concluded, that they have been on the whole ill-governed, or misgoverned, by their kings. Whereupon they say, more and more widely, 'let us henceforth have no kings; and no government at all.'

Now we said, we must face the full truth of the matter, in order to see what we are to do. And the truth is that the people *have* been misgoverned ;—that very little is to be said, hitherto, for most of their masters—and that certainly in many places they will try their new system of 'no masters': —and as that arrangement will be delightful to all foolish persons, and, at first, profitable to all wicked ones,—and as these classes are not wanting or unimportant in any human society,—the experiment is likely to be tried extensively. And the world may be quite content to endure much suffering with this fresh hope, and retain its faith in anarchy, whatever comes of it, till it can endure no more.

136. Then, secondly. The people have begun to suspect that one particular form of this past misgovernment has been, that their masters have set them to do all the work, and have themselves taken all the wages. In a word, that what was called governing them, meant only wearing fine clothes, and living on good fare at their expense. And, I am sorry to say, the people are quite right in this opinion also. If you enquire into the vital fact of the matter, this you will find to be the constant structure of European society for the thousand years of the feudal system ; it was divided into

peasants who lived by working; priests who lived by begging; and knights who lived by pillaging; and as the luminous public mind becomes gradually cognizant of these facts, it will assuredly not suffer things to be altogether arranged that way any more; and the devising of other ways will be an agitating business; especially because the first impression of the intelligent populace is, that whereas, in the dark ages, half the nation lived idle, in the bright ages to come, the whole of it may.

137. Now, thirdly—and here is much the worst phase of the crisis. This past system of misgovernment, especially during the last three hundred years, has prepared, by its neglect, a class among the lower orders which it is now peculiarly difficult to govern. It deservedly lost their respect—but that was the least part of the mischief. The deadly part of it was, that the lower orders lost their habit, and at last their faculty, of respect;—lost the very capability of reverence, which is the most precious part of the human soul. Exactly in the degree in which you can find creatures greater than yourself, to look up to, in that degree, you are ennobled yourself, and, in that degree, happy. If you could live always in the presence of archangels, you would be happier than in that of men; but even if only in the company of admirable knights and beautiful ladies, the more

noble and bright they were, and the more you could reverence their virtue, the happier you would be. On the contrary, if you were condemned to live among a multitude of idiots, dumb, distorted and malicious, you would not be happy in the constant sense of your own superiority. Thus, all real joy and power of progress in humanity depend on finding something to reverence; and all the baseness and misery of humanity, begin in a habit of disdain. Now, by general misgovernment, I repeat, we have created in Europe a vast populace, and out of Europe a still vaster one, which has lost even the power and conception of reverence;*—which exists only in the worship of itself—which can neither see anything beautiful around it, nor conceive anything virtuous above it; which has, towards all goodness and greatness, no other feelings than those of the lowest creatures—fear, hatred, or hunger: a populace which has sunk below your appeal in their nature, as it has risen beyond your power in their multitude;—whom you can now no more charm than you can the adder, nor discipline, than you can the summer fly.

It is a crisis, gentlemen; and time to think of it. I have roughly and broadly put it before you in its darkness. Let us look what we may find of light.

138. Only the other day, in a journal which is a

* Compare *Time and Tide*, § 169, and *Fors Clavigera*, Letter XIV. page 9.

fairly representative exponent of the Conservatism of our day, and for the most part not at all in favour of strikes or other popular proceedings; only about three weeks since, there was a leader, with this, or a similar, title—'What is to become of the House of Lords?' It startled me, for it seemed as if we were going even faster than I had thought, when such a question was put as a subject of quite open debate, in a journal meant chiefly for the reading of the middle and upper classes. Open or not—the debate is near. What *is* to become of them? And the answer to such question depends first on their being able to answer another question—'What is the *use* of them!' For some time back, I think the theory of the nation has been, that they are useful as impediments to business, so as to give time for second thoughts. But the nation is getting impatient of impediments to business; and certainly, sooner or later, will think it needless to maintain these expensive obstacles to its humours. And I have not heard, either in public, or from any of themselves, a clear expression of their own conception of their use. So that it seems thus to become needful for all men to tell them, as our one quite clear-sighted teacher, Carlyle, has been telling us for many a year, that the use of the Lords of a country is to *govern* the country. If they answer that use, the country will rejoice in keeping them; if not, that will become of them which must of all things found to have lost their serviceableness.

139. Here, therefore, is the one question, at this crisis, for them, and for us. Will they be lords indeed, and give us laws—dukes indeed, and give us guiding—princes indeed, and give us beginning, of truer dynasty, which shall not be soiled by covetousness, nor disordered by iniquity? Have they themselves sunk so far as not to hope this? Are there yet any among them who can stand forward with open English brows, and say,—So far as in me lies, I will govern with my might, not for Dieu et *mon* Droit, but for the first grand reading of the war cry, from which that was corrupted, 'Dieu et Droit.' Among them I know there are some—among you, soldiers of England, I know there are many, who can do this; and in you is our trust. I, one of the lower people of your country, ask of you in their name,—you whom I will not any more call soldiers, but by the truer name of Knights;—Equites of England. How many yet of you are there, knights errant now beyond all former fields of danger—knights patient now beyond all former endurance; who still retain the ancient and eternal purpose of knighthood, to subdue the wicked, and aid the weak? To them, be they few or many, we English people call for help to the

wretchedness, and for rule over the baseness, of multitudes desolate and deceived, shrieking to one another this new gospel of their new religion. 'Let the weak do as they can, and the wicked as they will.'

140. I can hear you saying in your hearts, even the bravest of you, 'The time is past for all that.' Gentlemen, it is not so. The time has come for *more* than all that. Hitherto, soldiers have given their lives for false fame, and for cruel power. The day is now when they must give their lives for true fame, and for beneficent power; and the work is near every one of you—close beside you—the means of it even thrust into your hands. The people are crying to you for command, and you stand there at pause, and silent. You think they don't want to be commanded; try them; determine what is needful for them—honourable for them; show it them, promise to bring them to it, and they will follow you through fire. 'Govern us,' they cry with one heart, though many minds. They *can* be governed still, these English; they are men still; not gnats, nor serpents. They love their old ways yet, and their old masters, and their old land. They would fain live in it, as many as may stay there, if you will show them how, there, to live;—or show them even, how, there, like Englishmen, to die.

141. 'To live in it, as many as may!' How

many do you think may? How many *can?* How many do you want to live there? As masters, your first object must be to increase your power; and in what does the power of a country consist? Will you have dominion over its stones, or over its clouds, or over its souls? What do you mean by a great nation, but a great multitude of men who are true to each other, and strong, and of worth? Now you can increase the multitude only definitely—your island has only so much standing room—but you can increase the *worth in*definitely. It is but a little island;—suppose, little as it is, you were to fill it with friends? You may, and that easily. You must, and that speedily; or there will be an end to this England of ours, and to all its loves and enmities.

142. To fill this little island with true friends—men brave, wise, and happy! Is it so impossible, think you, after the world's eighteen hundred years of Christianity, and our own thousand years of toil, to fill only this little white gleaming crag with happy creatures, helpful to each other? Africa, and India, and the Brazilian wide-watered plain, are these not wide enough for the ignorance of our race? have they not space enough for its pain? Must we remain *here* also savage,—*here* at enmity with each other,—*here* foodless, houseless, in rags, in dust, and without hope, as thousands and tens of thousands of us are

lying? Do not think it, gentlemen. The thought that it is inevitable is the last infidelity; infidelity not to God only, but to every creature and every law that He has made. Are we to think that the earth was only shaped to be a globe of torture; and that there cannot be one spot of it where peace can rest, or justice reign? Where are men ever to be happy, if not in England? by whom shall they ever be taught to do right, if not by you? Are we not of a race first among the strong ones of the earth; the blood in us incapable of weariness, unconquerable by grief? Have we not a history of which we can hardly think without becoming insolent in our just pride of it? Can we dare, without passing every limit of courtesy to other nations, to say how much more we have to be proud of in our ancestors than they? Among our ancient monarchs, great crimes stand out as monstrous and strange. But their valour, and, according to their understanding, their benevolence, are constant. The Wars of the Roses, which are as a fearful crimson shadow on our land, represent the normal condition of other nations; while from the days of the Heptarchy downwards we have had examples given us, in all ranks, of the most varied and exalted virtue; a heap of treasure that no moth can corrupt, and which even our traitorship, if we are to become traitors to it, cannot sully.

143. And this is the race, then, that we know not any more how to govern! and this the history which we are to behold broken off by sedition! and this is the country, of all others, where life is to become difficult to the honest, and ridiculous to the wise! And the catastrophe, forsooth, is to come just when we have been making swiftest progress beyond the wisdom and wealth of the past. Our cities are a wilderness of spinning wheels instead of palaces; yet the people have not clothes. We have blackened every leaf of English greenwood with ashes, and the people die of cold; our harbours are a forest of merchant ships, and the people die of hunger.

Whose fault is it? Yours, gentlemen; yours only. You alone can feed them, and clothe, and bring into their right minds, for you only can govern—that is to say, you only can educate them.

144. Educate, or govern, they are one and the same word. Education does not mean teaching people to know what they do not know. It means teaching them to behave as they do not behave. And the true 'compulsory education' which the people now ask of you is not catechism, but drill. It is not teaching the youth of England the shapes of letters and the tricks of numbers; and then leaving them to turn their arithmetic to roguery, and their literature to lust. It is, on the contrary, training

them into the perfect exercise and kingly continence of their bodies and souls. It is a painful, continual, and difficult work; to be done by kindness, by watching, by warning, by precept, and by praise,—but above all—by example.

145. Compulsory! Yes, by all means! 'Go ye out into the highways and hedges, and *compel* them to come in.' Compulsory! Yes, and gratis also. *Dei Gratia*, they must be taught, as, *Dei Gratia*, you are set to teach them. I hear strange talk continually, 'how difficult it is to make people pay for being educated!' Why, I should think so! Do you make your children pay for their education, or do you give it them compulsorily, and gratis? You do not expect *them* to pay you for their teaching, except by becoming good children. Why should you expect a peasant to pay for his, except by becoming a good man?—payment enough, I think, if we knew it. Payment enough to himself, as to us. For that is another of our grand popular mistakes—people are always thinking of education as a means of livelihood. Education is not a profitable business, but a costly one; nay, even the best attainments of it are always unprofitable, in any terms of coin. No nation ever made its bread either by its great arts, or its great wisdoms. By its minor arts or manufactures, by its practical knowledges, yes: but its noble

scholarship, its noble philosophy, and its noble art, are always to be bought as a treasure, not sold for a livelihood. You do not learn that you may live—you live that you may learn. You are to spend on National Education, and to be spent for it, and to make by it, not more money, but better men;—to get into this British Island the greatest possible number of good and brave Englishmen. *They* are to be your 'money's worth.'

But where is the money to come from? Yes, that is to be asked. Let us, as quite the first business in this our national crisis, look not only into our affairs, but into our accounts, and obtain some general notion how we annually spend our money, and what we are getting for it. Observe, I do not mean to enquire into the public revenue only; of that some account is rendered already. But let us do the best we can to set down the items of the national *private* expenditure; and know what we spend altogether, and how.

146. To begin with this matter of education. You probably have nearly all seen the admirable lecture lately given by Captain Maxse, at Southampton. It contains a clear statement of the facts at present ascertained as to our expenditure in that respect. It appears that of our public moneys, for every pound that we spend on education we spend twelve either

in charity or punishment;—ten millions a year on pauperism and crime, and eight hundred thousand in instruction. Now Captain Maxse adds to this estimate of ten millions public money spent on crime and want, a more or less conjectural sum of eight millions for private charities. My impression is that this is much beneath the truth, but at all events it leaves out of consideration much the heaviest and saddest form of charity—the maintenance, by the working members of families, of the unfortunate or ill-conducted persons whom the general course of misrule now leaves helpless, to be the burden of the rest.

147. Now I want to get first at some, I do not say approximate, but at all events some suggestive, estimate of the quantity of real distress and misguided life in this country. Then next, I want some fairly representative estimate of our private expenditure in luxuries. We won't spend more, publicly, it appears, than eight hundred thousand a year, on educating men, gratis. I want to know, as nearly as possible, what we spend privately a year, in educating horses gratis. Let us, at least, quit ourselves in this from the taunt of Rabshakeh, and see that for every horse we train also a horseman; and that the rider be at least as high-bred as the horse, not jockey, but chevalier. Again, we spend eight hundred thousand, which is

certainly a great deal of money, in making rough *minds* bright. I want to know how much we spend annually in making rough *stones* bright; that is to say, what may be the united annual sum, or near it, of our jewellers' bills. So much we pay for educating children gratis;—how much for educating diamonds gratis? and which pays best for brightening, the spirit, or the charcoal? Let us get those two items set down with some sincerity, and a few more of the same kind. *Publicly* set down. We must not be ashamed of the way we spend our money. If our right hand is not to know what our left does, it must not be because it would be ashamed if it did.

That is, therefore, quite the first practical thing to be done. Let every man who wishes well to his country, render it yearly an account of his income, and of the main heads of his expenditure; or, if he is ashamed to do so, let him no more impute to the poor their poverty as a crime, nor set them to break stones in order to frighten them from committing it. To lose money ill is indeed often a crime; but to get it ill is a worse one, and to spend it ill, worst of all. You object, Lords of England, to increase, to the poor, the wages you give them, because they spend them, you say, unadvisedly. Render them, therefore, an account of the wages which *they* give *you;* and show them, by your example, how to spend theirs, to the last farthing, advisedly.

148. It is indeed time to make this an acknowledged subject of instruction to the working man,—how to spend his wages. For, gentlemen, we *must* give that instruction, whether we will or no, one way or the other. We have given it in years gone by; and now we find fault with our peasantry for having been too docile, and profited too shrewdly by our tuition. Only a few days since I had a letter from the wife of a village rector, a man of common sense and kindness, who was greatly troubled in his mind because it was precisely the men who got highest wages in summer that came destitute to his door in the winter. Destitute, and of riotous temper—for their method of spending wages in their period of prosperity was by sitting two days a week in the tavern parlour, ladling port wine, not out of bowls, but out of buckets. Well, gentlemen, who taught them that method of festivity? Thirty years ago, I, a most inexperienced freshman, went to my first college supper; at the head of the table sat a nobleman of high promise and of admirable powers, since dead of palsy; there also we had in the midst of us, not buckets, indeed, but bowls as large as buckets; there also, we helped ourselves with ladles. There (for this beginning of college education was compulsory), I

choosing ladlefuls of punch instead of claret, because I was then able, unperceived, to pour them into my waistcoat instead of down my throat, stood it out to the end, and helped to carry four of my fellow students, one of them the son of the head of a college, head foremost, down stairs and home.

149. Such things are no more; but the fruit of them remains, and will for many a day to come. The labourers whom you cannot now shut out of the alehouse are only the too faithful disciples of the gentlemen who were wont to shut themselves into the dining-room. The gentlemen have not thought it necessary, in order to correct their own habits, to diminish their incomes; and, believe me, the way to deal with your drunken workman is not to lower his wages,—but to mend his wits.*

150. And if indeed we do not yet see quite clearly how to deal with the sins of our poor brother, it is possible that our dimness of sight may still have other causes that can be cast out. There are two opposite cries of the great liberal and conservative parties, which are both most right, and worthy to be rallying cries. On their side 'let every man have his chance;' on yours 'let every man stand in his place.' Yes, indeed, let that be so, every man in his place,

* See Appendix, 'Modern Education,' and compare § 70 of *Time and Tide*.

and every man fit for it. See that he holds that place from Heaven's Providence; and not from his family's Providence. Let the Lords Spiritual quit themselves of simony, we laymen will look after the heretics for them. Let the Lords Temporal quit themselves of nepotism, and we will take care of their authority for them. Publish for us, you soldiers, an army gazette, in which the one subject of daily intelligence shall be the grounds of promotion; a gazette which shall simply tell us, what there certainly can be no detriment to the service in our knowing, when any officer is appointed to a new command,—what his former services and successes have been,—whom he has superseded,—and on what ground. It will be always a satisfaction to us; it may sometimes be an advantage to you: and then, when there is really necessary debate respecting reduction of wages, let us always begin, not with the wages of the industrious classes, but with those of the idle ones. Let there be honorary titles, if people like them; but let there be no honorary incomes.

151. So much for the master's motto, 'Every man in his place.' Next for the labourer's motto, 'Every man his chance.' Let us mend that for them a little, and say, 'Every man his certainty'—certainty, that if he does well, he will be honoured, and aided, and advanced in such degree as may be

fitting for his faculty and consistent with his peace; and equal certainty that if he does ill, he will by sure justice be judged, and by sure punishment be chastised; if it may be, corrected; and if that may not be, condemned. That is the right reading of the Republican motto, 'Every man his chance.' And then, with such a system of government, pure, watchful and just, you may approach your great problem of national education, or in other words, of national employment. For all education begins in work. What we think, or what we know, or what we believe, is in the end, of little consequence. The only thing of consequence is what we *do:* and for man, woman, or child, the first point of education is to make them do their best. It is the law of good economy to make the best of everything. How much more to make the best of every creature! Therefore, when your pauper comes to you and asks for bread, ask of him instantly—What faculty have you? What can you do best? Can you drive a nail into wood? Go and mend the parish fences. Can you lay a brick? Mend the walls of the cottages where the wind comes in. Can you lift a spadeful of earth? Turn this field up three feet deep all over. Can you only drag a weight with your shoulders? Stand at the bottom of this hill and help up the overladen horses. Can you weld iron and chisel stone? Fortify this wreck-strewn coast into a harbour; and change these shifting sands into fruitful ground. Wherever death was, bring life; that is to be your work; that your parish refuge; that your education. So and no otherwise can we meet existent distress. But for the continual education of the whole people, and for their future happiness, they must have such consistent employment as shall develop all the powers of the fingers and the limbs, and the brain; and that development is only to be obtained by hand-labour, of which you have these four great divisions—hand-labour on the earth, hand-labour on the sea, hand-labour in art, hand-labour in war. Of the last two of these I cannot speak to-night, and of the first two only with extreme brevity.

152. I. Hand-labour on the earth, the work of the husbandman and of the shepherd;—to dress the earth and to keep the flocks of it—the first task of man, and the final one—the education always of noblest lawgivers, kings and teachers; the education of Hesiod, of Moses, of David, of all the true strength of Rome; and all its tenderness: the pride of Cincinnatus, and the inspiration of Virgil. Hand-labour on the earth, and the harvest of it brought forth with singing:—not steam-piston labour on the earth, and the harvest of it brought forth with steam-whistling. You will have no prophet's voice accompanied by

that shepherd's pipe, and pastoral symphony. Do you know that lately, in Cumberland, in the chief pastoral district of England,—in Wordsworth's own home,—a procession of villagers on their festa day provided for themselves, by way of music, a steam-plough whistling at the head of them.

153. Give me patience while I put the principle of machine labour before you, as clearly and in as short compass as possible; it is one that should be known at this juncture. Suppose a farming proprietor needs to employ a hundred men on his estate, and that the labour of these hundred men is enough, but not more than enough, to till all his land, and to raise from it food for his own family, and for the hundred labourers. He is obliged under such circumstances to maintain all the men in moderate comfort, and can only by economy accumulate much for himself. But, suppose he contrive a machine that will easily do the work of fifty men, with only one man to watch it. This sounds like a great advance in civilization. The farmer of course gets his machine made, turns off the fifty men, who may starve or emigrate at their choice, and now he can keep half of the produce of his estate, which formerly went to feed them, all to himself. That is the essential and constant operation of machinery among us at this moment.

154. Nay, it is at first answered; no man can in reality keep half the produce of an estate to himself, nor can he in the end keep more than his own human share of anything; his riches must diffuse themselves at some time; he must maintain somebody else with them, however he spends them. That is mainly true (not altogether so), for food and fuel are in ordinary circumstances personally wasted by rich people, in quantities which would save many lives. One of my own great luxuries, for instance, is candlelight—and I probably burn, for myself alone, as many candles during the winter, as would comfort the old eyes, or spare the young ones, of a whole rushlighted country village. Still, it is mainly true that it is not by their personal waste that rich people prevent the lives of the poor. This is the way they do it. Let me go back to my farmer. He has got his machine made, which goes creaking, screaming, and occasionally exploding, about modern Arcadia. He has turned off his fifty men to starve. Now, at some distance from his own farm, there is another on which the labourers were working for their bread in the same way, by tilling the land. The machinist sends over to these, saying—'I have got food enough for you without your digging or ploughing any more. I can maintain you in other occupations instead of ploughing that land; if you rake in its gravel you will find

some hard stones—you shall grind those on mills till they glitter; then, my wife shall wear a necklace of them. Also, if you turn up the meadows below you will find some fine white clay, of which you shall make a porcelain service for me: and the rest of the farm I want for pasture for horses for my carriage—and you shall groom them, and some of you ride behind the carriage with staves in your hands, and I will keep you much fatter for doing that than you can keep yourselves by digging.'

155. Well—but it is answered, are we to have no diamonds, nor china, nor pictures, nor footmen, then —but all to be farmers? I am not saying what we ought to do, I want only to show you with perfect clearness first what we *are doing*; and that, I repeat, is the upshot of machine-contriving in this country. And observe its effect on the national strength. Without machines, you have a hundred and fifty yeomen ready to join for defence of the land. You get your machine, starve fifty of them, make diamond-cutters or footmen of as many more, and for your national defence against an enemy, you have now, and *can* have, only fifty men, instead of a hundred and fifty; these also now with minds much alienated from you as their chief,* and the rest, lapidaries or footmen;—and a steam plough.

* [They were deserting, I am informed, in the early part of this year, 1873, at the rate of a regiment a week.]

156. That is one effect of machinery; but at all events, if we have thus lost in men, we have gained in riches; instead of happy human souls, we have at least got pictures, china, horses, and are ourselves better off than we were before. But very often, and in much of our machine-contriving, even *that* result does not follow. We are not one whit the richer for the machine, we only employ it for our amusement. For observe, our gaining in riches depends on the men who are out of employment consenting to be starved, or sent out of the country. But suppose they do not consent passively to be starved, but some of them become criminals, and have to be taken charge of and fed at a much greater cost than if they were at work, and others, paupers, rioters, and the like, then you attain the real outcome of modern wisdom and ingenuity. You had your hundred men honestly at country work; but you don't like the sight of human beings in your fields; you like better to see a smoking kettle. You pay, as an amateur, for that pleasure, and you employ your fifty men in picking oakum, or begging, rioting, and thieving.

157. By hand-labour, therefore, and that alone, we are to till the ground. By hand-labour also to plough the sea; both for food, and in commerce, and in war: not with floating kettles there neither, but with hempen bridle, and the winds of heaven in

harness. That is the way the power of Greece rose on her Egean, the power of Venice on her Adria, of Amalfi in her blue bay, of the Norman sea-riders from the North Cape to Sicily:—so, your own dominion also of the past. Of the past mind you. On the Baltic and the Nile, your power is already departed. By machinery you would advance to discovery; by machinery you would carry your commerce;—you would be engineers instead of sailors; and instantly, in the North seas you are beaten among the ice, and before the very Gods of Nile, beaten among the sand. Agriculture, then, by the hand or by the plough drawn only by animals: and shepherd and pastoral husbandry, are to be the chief schools of Englishmen. And this most royal academy of all academies you have to open over all the land, purifying your heaths and hills, and waters, and keeping them full of every kind of lovely natural organism, in tree, herb, and living creature. All land that is waste and ugly, you must redeem into ordered fruitfulness; all ruin, desolateness, imperfectness of hut or habitation, you must do away with; and throughout every village and city of your English dominion, there must not be a hand that cannot find a helper, nor a heart that cannot find a comforter.

158. 'How impossible?' I know, you are thinking. Ah! So far from impossible, it is easy,

it is natural, it is necessary, and I declare to you that, sooner or later, it *must be done*, at our peril. If now our English lords of land will fix this idea steadily before them; take the people to their hearts, trust to their loyalty, lead their labour;—then indeed there will be princes again in the midst of us, worthy of the island throne,

> 'This royal throne of kings—this sceptred isle—
> This fortress built by nature for herself
> Against infection, and the hand of war;
> This precious stone set in the silver sea;
> This happy breed of men—this little world;
> This other Eden—Demi-Paradise.'

But if they refuse to do this, and hesitate and equivocate, clutching through the confused catastrophe of all things only at what they can still keep stealthily for themselves,—their doom is nearer than even their adversaries hope, and it will be deeper than even their despisers dream.

159. That, believe me, is the work you have to do in England; and out of England you have room for everything else you care to do. Are her dominions in the world so narrow that she can find no place to spin cotton in but Yorkshire? We may organize emigration into an infinite power. We may assemble troops of the more adventurous and ambitious of our youth; we may send them on truest foreign service, founding new seats of autho-

rity, and centres of thought, in uncultivated and unconquered lands; retaining the full affection to the native country no less in our colonists than in our armies, teaching them to maintain allegiance to their fatherland in labour no less than in battle; aiding them with free hand in the prosecution of discovery, and the victory over adverse natural powers; establishing seats of every manufacture in the climates and places best fitted for it, and bringing ourselves into due alliance and harmony of skill with the dexterities of every race, and the wisdoms of every tradition and every tongue.

160. And then you may make England itself the centre of the learning, of the arts, of the courtesies and felicities of the world. You may cover her mountains with pasture; her plains with corn, her valleys with the lily, and her gardens with the rose. You may bring together there in peace the wise and the pure, and the gentle of the earth, and by their word, command through its farthest darkness the birth of 'God's first creature, which was Light.' You know whose words those are; the words of the wisest of Englishmen. He, and with him the wisest of all other great nations, have spoken always to men of this hope, and they would not hear. Plato, in the dialogue of Critias, his last, broken off at his death,—Pindar, in passionate singing of the

fortunate islands,—Virgil, in the prophetic tenth eclogue,—Bacon, in his fable of the New Atlantis,—More, in the book which, too impatiently wise, became the bye-word of fools—these, all, have told us with one voice what we should strive to attain; *they* not hopeless of it, but for our follies forced, as it seems, by heaven, to tell us only partly and in parables, lest we should hear them and obey.

Shall we never listen to the words of these wisest of men. Then listen at least to the words of your children—let us in the lips of babes and sucklings find our strength; and see that we do not make them mock instead of pray, when we teach them, night and morning, to ask for what we believe never can be granted;—that the will of the Father,—which is, that his creatures may be righteous and happy,—should be done, *on earth*, as it is in Heaven.

APPENDIX.

APPENDIX.

NOTES ON THE POLITICAL ECONOMY OF PRUSSIA.

I AM often accused of inconsistency; but believe myself defensible against the charge with respect to what I have said on nearly every subject except that of war. It is impossible for me to write consistently of war, for the groups of facts I have gathered about it lead me to two precisely opposite conclusions.

When I find this the case, in other matters, I am silent, till I can choose my conclusion: but, with respect to war, I am forced to speak, by the necessities of the time; and forced to act, one way or another. The conviction on which I act is, that it causes an incalculable amount of avoidable human suffering, and that it ought to cease among Christian nations; and if therefore any of my boy-friends desire to be soldiers, I try my utmost to bring them into what I conceive to be a better mind. But, on the other hand, I know certainly that the most beautiful characters yet developed among men have been formed in war;—that all great nations have been warrior nations, and that the only kinds of peace which we are likely to get in the present age are ruinous alike to the intellect, and the heart.

The last lecture, in this volume, addressed to young soldiers, had for its object to strengthen their trust in the virtue of their profession. It is inconsistent with itself, in its closing appeal to women, praying them to use their influence to bring wars to an end. And I have been hindered from completing my long intended notes on the economy of the Kings of Prussia by continually increasing doubt how far the machinery and discipline of war, under which they learned the art of government, was essential for such lesson; and what the honesty and sagacity of the Friedrich who so nobly repaired his ruined Prussia, might have done for the happiness of his Prussia, unruined.

In war, however, or in peace, the character which Carlyle chiefly loves him for, and in which Carlyle has shown him to differ from all kings up to this time succeeding him, is his constant purpose to use every power entrusted to him for the good of his people; and be, not in name only, but in heart and hand, their king.

Not in ambition, but in natural instinct of duty.

Friedrich, born to govern, determines to govern to the best of his faculty. That 'best' may sometimes be unwise; and self-will, or love of glory, may have their oblique hold on his mind, and warp it this way or that; but they are never principal with him. He believes that war is necessary, and maintains it; sees that peace is necessary, and calmly persists in the work of it to the day of his death, not claiming therein more praise than the head of any ordinary household, who rules it simply because it is his place, and he must not yield the mastery of it to another.

How far, in the future, it may be possible for men to gain the strength necessary for kingship without either fronting death, or inflicting it, seems to me not at present determinable. The historical facts are that, broadly speaking, none but soldiers, or persons with a soldierly faculty, have ever yet shown themselves fit to be kings; and that no other men are so gentle, so just, or so clear-sighted. Wordsworth's character of the happy warrior cannot be reached in the height of it *but by* a warrior; nay, so much is it beyond common strength that I had supposed the entire meaning of it to be metaphorical, until one of the best soldiers of England himself read me the poem,* and taught me, what I might have known, had I enough watched his own life, that it was

* The late Sir Herbert Edwardes.

entirely literal. There is nothing of so high reach distinctly demonstrable in Friedrich: but I see more and more, as I grow older, that the things which are the most worth, encumbered among the errors and faults of every man's nature, are never clearly demonstrable; and are often most forcible when they are scarcely distinct to his own conscience,—how much less, clamorous for recognition by others!

Nothing can be more beautiful than Carlyle's showing of this, to any careful reader of Friedrich. But careful readers are but one in the thousand; and by the careless, the masses of detail with which the historian must deal are insurmountable.

My own notes, made for the special purpose of hunting down the one point of economy, though they cruelly spoil Carlyle's own current and method of thought, may yet be useful in enabling readers, unaccustomed to books involving so vast a range of conception, to discern what, on this one subject only, may be gathered from that history. On any other subject of importance, similar gatherings might be made of other passages. The historian has to deal with all at once.

I therefore have determined to print here, as a sequel to the Essay on War, my notes from the first volume of Friedrich, on the economies of Brandenburg, up to the date of the establishment of the Prussian monarchy. The economies of the first three Kings of Prussia I shall then take up in *Fors Clavigera*, finding them fitter for examination in connection with the subject of that book than of this.

I assume, that the reader will take down his first volume of Carlyle, and read attentively the passages to which I refer him. I give the reference first to the largest edition, in six volumes (1858–1865); then, in parenthesis, to the smallest or 'people's edition' (1872–1873). The pieces which I have quoted in my own text are for the use of readers who may not have ready access to the book; and are enough for the explanation of the points to which I wish them to direct their thoughts in reading such histories of soldiers or soldier-kingdoms.

I.

Year 928 to 936.—*Dawn of Order in Christian Germany.*

Book II. Chap. i. p. 67 (47).

HENRY THE FOWLER, 'the beginning of German kings,' is a mighty soldier *in the cause of peace*; his essential work the building and organization of fortified towns for the protection of men.

Read page 72 with utmost care (51), 'He fortified towns,' to end of small print. I have added some notes on the matter in my lecture on Giovanni Pisano; but whether you can glance at them or not, fix in your mind this institution of truly civil or civic building in Germany, as distinct from the building of baronial castles for the security of *robbers*: and of a standing army consisting of every ninth man, called a 'burgher' ('townsman')—a soldier, appointed to learn that profession that he may guard the walls—the exact reverse of *our* notion of a burgher.

Frederick's final idea of his army is, indeed, only this.

Brannibor, a chief fortress of the Wends, is thus taken, and further strengthened by Henry the Fowler; wardens appointed for it; and thus the history of Brandenburg begins. On all frontiers, also, this 'beginning of German kings' has his 'Markgraf.' 'Ancient of the marked place.' Read page 73, measuredly, learning it by heart, if it may be. (51-2.)

II.

936–1000.—*History of Nascent Brandenburg.*

THE passage I last desired you to read ends with this sentence: "The sea-wall you build, and what main floodgates you establish in it, will depend on the state of the outer sea."

From this time forward you have to keep clearly separate in your minds, (A) the history of that outer sea, Pagan Scandinavia, Russia, and Bor-Russia, or Prussia proper; (B) the history of Henry the Fowler's Eastern and Western Marches; asserting themselves gradually as Austria and the Netherlands; and (C) the history of this inconsiderable fortress of Brandenburg, gradually becoming considerable, and the capital city of increasing district between them. That last history, however, Carlyle is obliged to leave vague and gray for two hundred years after Henry's death. Absolutely dim for the first century, in which nothing is evident but that its wardens or Markgraves had no peaceable possession of the place. Read the second paragraph in page 74 (52–3), 'in old books' to 'reader,' and the first in page 83 (59), 'meanwhile' to 'substantial,' consecutively. They bring the story of Brandenburg itself down, at any rate, from 936 to 1000.

III.

936–1000.—*State of the Outer Sea.*

READ now Chapter II. beginning at page 76 (54), wherein you will get account of the beginning of vigorous missionary work on the outer sea, in Prussia proper; of the death of St. Adalbert, and of the purchase of his dead body by the Duke of Poland.

You will not easily understand Carlyle's laugh in this chapter, unless you have learned yourself to laugh in sadness, and to laugh in love.

'No Czech blows his pipe in the woodlands without certain precautions and preliminary fuglings of a devotional nature.' (Imagine St. Adalbert, in spirit, at the railway station in Birmingham !)

My own main point for notice in the chapter is the purchase of his body for its 'weight in gold.' Swindling angels held it up in the scales ; it did not weigh so much as a web of gossamer. 'Had such excellent odour, too, and came for a mere nothing of gold,' says Carlyle. It is one of the first commercial transactions of Germany, but I regret the conduct of the angels on the occasion. Evangelicalism has been proud of ceasing to invest in relics, its swindling angels helping it to better things, as it supposes. For my own part, I believe Christian Germany could not have bought at this time any treasure more precious ; nevertheless, the missionary work itself you find is wholly vain. The difference of opinion between St. Adalbert and the Wends, on divine matters, does not signify to the Fates. They will not have it disputed about ; and end the dispute adversely to St. Adalbert,—adversely, even, to Brandenburg and its civilising power, as you will immediately see.

IV.

1000–1030.—*History of Brandenburg in Trouble.*

Book II. Chap. iii. p. 83 (59).

THE adventures of Brandenburg in contest with Pagan Prussia, irritated, rather than amended, by St.

Adalbert. In 1023, roughly, a hundred years after Henry the Fowler's death, Brandenburg is taken by the Wends, and its first line of Markgraves ended; its population mostly butchered, especially the priests; and the Wend's God, Triglaph, 'something like three whales' cubs combined by boiling,' set up on the top of St. Mary's Hill.

Here is an adverse 'Doctrine of the Trinity' which has its supporters! It is wonderful,—this Tripod and Triglyph,—three-footed, three-cut faith of the North and South, the leaf of the oxalis, and strawberry, and clover, fostering the same in their simple manner. I suppose it to be the most savage and natural of notions about Deity: a prismatic idol-shape of Him, rude as a triangular log, as a trefoil grass. I do not find how long Triglaph held his state on St. Mary's Hill. 'For a time,' says Carlyle, 'the priests all slain or fled,—shadowy Markgraves the like—church and state lay in ashes, and Triglaph, like a triple porpoise under the influence of laudanum, stood, I know not whether on his head or his tail, aloft on the Harlungsberg, as the Supreme of this Universe for the time being.'

V.

1030–1130.—*Brandenburg under the Ditmarsch Markgraves, or Ditmarsch-Stade Markgraves.*

Book II. Chap. iii. p. 85 (60).

OF Anglish, or Saxon breed. They attack Brandenburg, under its Triglyphic protector, take it—dethrone him, and hold the town for a hundred years, their history 'stamped beneficially on the face of things, Markgraf after Markgraf getting killed in the business. "Erschlagen," "slain," fighting with the Heathen —say the old books, and pass on to another.' If we allow seven years to Triglaph—we get a clear century for these—as above indicated. They die out in 1130.

VI.

1130–1170.—*Brandenburg under Albert the Bear.*

Book II. Chap iv. p. 91 (64).

HE is the first of the Ascanien Markgraves, whose castle of Ascanien is on the northern slope of the Hartz Mountains, 'ruins still dimly traceable.'

There had been no soldier or king of note among the Ditmarsch Markgraves, so that you will do well to fix in your mind successively the three men, Henry the Fowler, St. Adalbert, and Albert the Bear. A soldier again, and a strong one. Named the Bear only from the device on his shield, first wholly definite Markgraf of Brandenburg that there is, 'and that the luckiest of events for Brandenburg.' Read page 93 (66) carefully, and note this of his economies.

Nothing better is known to me of Albert the Bear than his introducing large numbers of Dutch Netherlanders into those countries; men thrown out of work, who already knew how to deal with bog and sand, by mixing and delving, and who first taught Brandenburg what greenness and cow-pasture was. The Wends, in presence of such things, could not but consent more and more to efface themselves—either to become German, and grow milk and cheese in the Dutch manner, or to disappear from the world.

* * * * * *

After two-hundred and fifty years of barking and worrying, the Wends are now finally reduced to silence; their anarchy well buried and wholesome Dutch cabbage planted over it; Albert did several great things in the world; but this, for posterity, remains his memorable feat. Not done quite easily, but done: big destinies of nations or of persons are not founded gratis in this world. He had a sore, toilsome time of it, coercing, warring, managing among his fellow-creatures, while his day's work lasted—fifty years or so, for it began early. He died in his Castle of Ballenstädt, peaceably among the Hartz Mountains at last, in the year 1170, age about sixty-five.

Now, note in all this the steady gain of soldiership enforcing order and agriculture, with St. Adalbert giving higher strain to the imagination. Henry the Fowler establishes walled towns, fighting for mere peace. Albert the Bear plants the country with cabbages, fighting for his cabbage-fields. And the disciples of St. Adalbert, generally, have succeeded in substituting some idea of Christ for the idea of Triglaph. Some idea only; other ideas than of Christ haunt even to this day those Hartz Mountains among which Albert the Bear dies so peacefully. Mephistopheles, and all his ministers, inhabit there, commanding mephitic clouds and earth-born dreams.

VII.

1170–1320.—*Brandenburg 150 years under the Ascanien Markgraves.*

Vol. I. Book II. Chap. viii. p. 135 (96).

'Wholesome Dutch cabbages continued to be more and more planted by them in the waste sand: intrusive chaos, and Triglaph held at bay by them,' till at last in 1240, seventy years after the great Bear's death, they fortify a new Burg, a '*little* rampart,' Wehrlin, diminutive of Wehr (or vallum), gradually smoothing itself, with a little echo of the Bear in it too, into Ber-lin, the oily river Spree flowing by, 'in which you catch various fish;' while trade over the flats and by the dull streams, is widely possible. Of the Ascanien race, the notablest is Otto with the Arrow, whose story see, pp. 138–141 (98–100), noting that Otto is one of the first Minnesingers; that, being a prisoner to the Archbishop of Magdeburg, his wife rescues him, selling her jewels to bribe the canons; and that the Knight, set free on parole and promise of farther ransom, rides back with his own price in his hand; holding himself thereat cheaply bought, though no angelic legerdemain happens to the scales now. His own estimate of his price—'Rain gold ducats on my war-horse and me, till you cannot see the point of my spear atop.'

Emptiness of utter pride, you think?

Not so. Consider with yourself, reader, how much you dare to say, aloud, *you* are worth. If you have *no* courage to name any price whatsoever for yourself, believe me, the cause is not your modesty, but that in very truth you feel in your heart there would be no bid for you at Lucian's sale of lives, were that again possible, at Christie and Manson's.

Finally (1319 exactly; say 1320, for memory), the Ascanien line expired in Brandenburg, and the little town and its electorate lapsed to the Kaiser: meantime other economical arrangements had been in progress; but observe first how far we have got.

The Fowler, St. Adalbert, and the Bear have established order, and some sort of Christianity; but the established persons begin to think somewhat too well of themselves. On quite honest terms, a dead saint or a living knight ought to be worth their true 'weight in gold.' But a pyramid, with only the point of the spear seen at top would be many times over one's weight in gold. And although men were yet far enough from the notion of modern days, that the gold is better than the flesh, and from buying it with the clay of one's body, and even the fire of one's soul, instead of soul and body with *it*, they were beginning to fight for their own supremacy, or for their own religious fancies, and not at all to any useful end, until an entirely unexpected movement is made in the old useful direction—forsooth, only by some kind ship-captains of Lübeck!

VIII.

1210–1320.—*Civil work, aiding military, during the Ascanien period.*

Vol. I. Book II. Chap. vi. p. 109 (77).

In the year 1190, Acre not yet taken, and the crusading army wasting by murrain on the shore, the German soldiers especially having none to look after them, certain compassionate ship-captains of Lübeck, one Walpot von Bassenheim taking the lead, formed themselves into an union for succour of the sick and the dying, set up canvas tents from the Lübeck ship stores, and did what utmost was in them silently in the name of mercy and heaven. Finding its work prosper, the little medicinal and weather-fending company took vows on itself, strict chivalry forms, and decided to become permanent 'Knights Hospitallers of our dear Lady of Mount Zion,' separate from the former Knights Hospitallers, as being entirely German: yet soon, as the German Order of St. Mary, eclipsing in importance Templars, Hospitallers, and every other chivalric order then extant; no purpose of battle in them, but much strength for it; their purpose only the helping of German pilgrims. To this only they are bound by their vow, 'gelübde,' and become one of the usefullest of clubs in all the Pall Mall of Europe.

Finding pilgrimage in Palestine falling slack, and more need for them on the homeward side of the sea, their Hochmeister, Hermann of the Salza, goes over to Venice in 1210. There, the titular bishop of still unconverted Preussen advises him of that field of work for his idle knights. Hermann thinks well of it: sets his St. Mary's riders at Triglaph, with the sword in one hand and a missal in the other.

Not your modern way of effecting conversion! Too

illiberal, you think; and what would Mr. J. S. Mill say?

But if Triglaph *had* been verily 'three whales' cubs combined by boiling,' you would yourself have promoted attack upon him for the sake of his oil, would not you? The Teutsch Ritters, fighting him for charity, are they so much inferior to you?

They built, and burnt, innumerable stockades for and against; built wooden forts which are now stone towns. They fought much and prevalently; galloped desperately to and fro, ever on the alert. In peaceabler ulterior times, they fenced in the Nogat and the Weichsel with dams, whereby unlimited quagmire might become grassy meadow—as it continues to this day. Marienburg (Mary's Burg), with its grand stone Schloss still visible and even habitable: this was at length their head-quarter. But how many Burgs of wood and stone they built, in different parts; what revolts, surprisals, furious fights in woody, boggy places they had, no man has counted.

But always some preaching by zealous monks, accompanied the chivalrous fighting. And colonists came in from Germany; trickling in, or at times streaming. Victorious Ritterdom offers terms to the beaten heathen: terms not of tolerant nature, but which *will be punctually kept by Ritterdom.* When the flame of revolt or general conspiracy burnt up again too extensively, high personages came on crusade to them. Ottocar, King of Bohemia, with his extensive far-shining chivalry, 'conquered Samland in a month;' tore up the Romova where Adalbert had been massacred, and burnt it from the face of the earth. A certain fortress was founded at that time, in Ottocar's presence; and in honour of him they named it King's Fortress, 'Königsberg.' Among King Ottocar's esquires, or subaltern junior officials, on this occasion, is one Rudolf, heir of a poor Swiss lordship and gray hill castle, called Hapsburg, rather in reduced circumstances, whom Ottocar likes for his prudent, hardy ways; a stout, modest, wise young man, who may chance to redeem Hapsburg a little, if he lives.

Conversion, and complete conquest once come, there was a happy time for Prussia; ploughshare instead of sword; busy sea-havens, German towns, getting built; churches everywhere rising; grass growing, and peaceable cows, where formerly had been quagmire and snakes, and for the Order a happy time. On the whole, this Teutsch Ritterdom, for the first century and more, was a grand phenomenon, and flamed like a bright blessed beacon through the night of things, in those Northern countries. For above a century, we perceive, it was the rallying place of all brave men who had a career to seek on terms other than vulgar. The noble soul, aiming beyond money, and sensible to more than hunger in this world, had a beacon burning (as we say), if the night chanced to overtake it, and the earth to grow too intricate, as is not uncommon. Better than the career of stump-oratory, I should fancy, and its Hesperides apples, golden, and of gilt horse-dung. Better than puddling away one's poor spiritual gift of God (loan, not gift), such as it may be, in building the lofty rhyme, the lofty review article, for a discerning public that has sixpence to spare! Times alter greatly.*

We must pause here again for a moment to think

* I would much rather print these passages of Carlyle in large golden letters than small black ones; but they are only here at all for unlucky people who can't read them with the context.

where we are, and who is *with us*. The Teutsch Ritters have been fighting, independently of all states, for their own hand, or St. Adalbert's;—partly for mere love of fight, partly for love of order, partly for love of God. Meantime, other Riders have been fighting wholly for what they could get by it; and other persons, not Riders, have not been fighting at all, but in their own towns peacefully manufacturing and selling.

Of Henry the Fowler's Marches, Austria has become a military power, Flanders a mercantile one, pious only in the degree consistent with their several occupations. Prussia is now a practical and farming country, more Christian than its longer-converted neighbours.

Towns are built, Königsberg (King Ottocar's town), Thoren (Thorn, City of the Gates), with many others; so that the wild population and the tame now lived tolerably together, under Gospel and Lübeck law; and all was ploughing and trading.

But Brandenburg itself, what of it?

The Ascanien Markgraves rule it on the whole prosperously down to 1320, when their line expires, and it falls into the power of Imperial Austria.

IX.

1320–1415.—*Brandenburg under the Austrians.*

A CENTURY—the fourteenth—of miserable anarchy and decline for Brandenburg, its Kurfürsts, in deadly succession, making what they can out of it for their own pockets. The city itself and its territory utterly helpless. Read pp. 180, 181 (129, 130). 'The towns suffered much, any trade they might have had going to wreck. Robber castles flourished, all else decayed, no highway safe. What are Hamburg pedlars made for but to be robbed?'

X.

1415–1440.—*Brandenburg under Friedrich of Nüremberg.*

THIS is the fourth of the men whom you are to remember as creators of the Prussian monarchy, Henry the Fowler, St. Adalbert, Albert the Bear, of Ascanien, and Friedrich of Nüremberg; (of Hohenzollern, by name, and by country, of the Black Forest, north of the Lake of Constance).

Brandenburg is sold to him at Constance, during the great Council, for about 200,000*l.* of our money, worth perhaps a million in that day; still, with its capabilities, 'dog cheap.' Admitting, what no one at the time denied, the general marketableness of states as private property, this is the one practical result, thinks Carlyle, (not likely to think wrong), of that œcumenical deliberation, four years long, of the 'elixir of the intellect and dignity of Europe. And that one thing was not its doing; but a pawnbroking job, intercalated,' putting, however, at last, Brandenburg again under the will of one strong man. On St. John's day, 1412, he first set foot in his town, 'and Brandenburg, under its wise Kurfürst, begins to be cosmic again.' The story of Heavy Peg, pages 195–198 (138, 140), is one of the most brilliant and important passages of the first volume; page 199, specially to our purpose, must be given entire:—

The offer to be Kaiser was made him in his old days; but he wisely declined that too. It was in Brandenburg, by what he silently founded there, that he did his chief benefit to Germany and mankind. He understood the noble art of governing men; had in him the justice, clearness, valour, and patience needed for that. A man of sterling probity, for one thing. *Which indeed is the first requisite in said art*:—if you will have your laws obeyed without mutiny, see well that they be pieces of God Almighty's law; otherwise all the artillery in the world will not keep down mutiny.

Friedrich 'travelled much over Brandenburg;' looking into everything with his own eyes; making, I can well fancy, innumerable crooked things straight; reducing more and more that famishing dog-kennel of a Brandenburg into a fruitful arable field. His portraits represent a square-headed, mild-looking, solid gentleman, with a certain twinkle of mirth in the serious eyes of him. Except in those Hussite wars for Kaiser Sigismund and the Reich, in which no man could prosper, he may be defined as constantly prosperous. To Brandenburg he was, very literally, the blessing of blessings; redemption out of death into life. In the ruins of that old Friesack Castle, battered down by Heavy Peg, antiquarian science (if it had any eyes) might look for the taproot of the Prussian nation, and the beginning of all that Brandenburg has since grown to under the sun.

Which growth is now traced by Carlyle in its various budding and withering, under the succession of the twelve Electors, of whom Friedrich, with his heavy Peg, is first, and Friedrich, first King of Prussia, grandfather of Friedrich the Great, the twelfth.

XI.

1415–1701.—*Brandenburg under the Hohenzollern Kurfürsts.*

Book III.

WHO the Hohenzollerns were, and how they came to power in Nüremberg, is told in Chap. v. of Book II.

Their succession in Brandenburg is given in brief at page 377 (269). I copy it, in absolute barrenness of enumeration, for our momentary convenience, here:

Friedrich 1st of Brandenburg (6th of Nüremberg),	1412–1440
Friedrich II., called 'Iron Teeth,'	1440–1472
Albert, ...	1472–1486
Johann, ...	1486–1499
Joachim I., ...	1499–1535
Joachim II., ...	1535–1571
Johann George, ...	1571–1598
Joachim Friedrich, ...	1598–1608
Johann Sigismund, ...	1608–1619
George Wilhelm, ...	1619–1640
Friedrich Wilhelm (the Great Elector), .	1640–1688
Friedrich, first King ; crowned 18th January, .	1701

Of this line of princes we have to say they followed generally in their ancestor's steps, and had success of the like kind, more or less ; Hohenzollerns all of them, by character and behaviour as well as by descent. No lack of quiet energy, of thrift, sound sense. There was likewise solid fair-play in general, no founding of yourself on ground that will not carry, *and there was instant, gentle, but inexorable crushing of mutiny*, if it showed itself, which, after the Second Elector, or at most the Third, it had altogether ceased to do.

This is the general account of them ; of special matters note the following :—

II. Friedrich, called 'Iron-teeth,' from his firmness, proves a notable manager and governor. Builds the palace at Berlin in its first form, and makes it his chief residence. Buys Neumark from the fallen Teutsch Ritters, and generally establishes things on securer footing.

III. Albert, 'a fiery, tough old gentleman,' called

the Achilles of Germany in his day; has half-a-century of fighting with his own Nürembergers, with Bavaria, France, Burgundy, and its fiery Charles, besides being head constable to the Kaiser among any disorderly persons in the East. His skull, long shown on his tomb, 'marvellous for strength and with no visible sutures.'

IV. John, the orator of his race; (but the orations unrecorded). His second son, Archbishop of Maintz, for whose piece of memorable work see page 223 (143) and read in connection with that the history of Margraf George, pp. 237–241 (152–154), and the 8th chapter of the third book.

V. Joachim I., of little note; thinks there has been enough Reformation, and checks proceedings in a dull stubbornness, causing him at least grave domestic difficulties.—Page 271 (173).

VI. Joachim II. Again active in the Reformation, and staunch,

though generally in a cautious, weighty, never in a rash, swift way, to the great cause of Protestantism, and to all good causes. He was himself a solemnly devout man; deep, awe-stricken reverence dwelling in his view of this universe. Most serious, though with a jocose dialect, commonly having a cheerful wit in speaking to men. Luther's books he called his Seelenschatz, (soul's treasure); Luther and the Bible were his chief reading. Fond of profane learning, too, and of the useful or ornamental arts; given to music, and 'would himself sing aloud' when he had a melodious leisure hour.

VII. Johann George, a prudent thrifty Herr; no mistresses, no luxuries allowed; at the sight of a new-fashioned coat he would fly out on an unhappy youth and pack him from his presence. Very strict in point of justice; a peasant once appealing to him in one of his inspection journeys through the country—

'Grant me justice, Durchlaucht, against so and so; I am your Highness's born subject.' 'Thou shouldst have it, man, wert thou a born Turk!' answered Johann George.

Thus, generally, we find this line of Electors representing in Europe the Puritan mind of England in a somewhat duller, but less dangerous, form; receiving what Protestantism could teach of honesty and common sense, but not its anti-Catholic fury, or its selfish spiritual anxiety. Pardon of sins is not to be had from Tetzel; neither, the Hohenzollern mind advises with itself, from even Tetzel's master, for either the buying, or the asking. On the whole, we had better commit as few as possible, and live just lives and plain ones.

A conspicuous thrift, veracity, modest solidity, looks through the conduct of this Herr; a determined Protestant he too, as indeed all the following were and are.

VIII. Joachim Friedrich. Gets hold of Prussia,

which hitherto, you observe, has always been spoken of as a separate country from Brandenburg. March 11, 1605—'Squeezed his way into the actual guardianship of Preussen and its imbecile Duke, which was his by right.'

For my own part, I do not trouble myself much about these rights, never being able to make out any single one, to begin with, except the right to keep everything and every place about you in as good order as you can—Prussia, Poland, or what else. I should much like, for instance, just now, to hear of any honest Cornish gentleman of the old Drake breed taking a fancy to land in Spain, and trying what he could make of his rights as far round Gibraltar as he could enforce them. At all events, Master Joachim has somehow got hold of Prussia; and means to keep it.

IX. Johann Sigismund. Only notable for our economical purposes, as getting the 'guardianship' of Prussia confirmed to him. The story at page 317 (226), 'a strong flame of choler,' indicates a new order of things among the knights of Europe—'princely etiquettes melting all into smoke.' Too literally so, that being one of the calamitous functions of the plain lives we are living, and of the busy life our country is living. In the Duchy of Cleve, specially, concerning which legal dispute begins in

Sigismund's time. And it is well worth the lawyers' trouble, it seems.

It amounted, perhaps, to two Yorkshires in extent. A naturally opulent country of fertile meadows, shipping capabilities, metalliferous hills, and at this time, in consequence of the Dutch-Spanish war, and the multitude of Protestant refugees, it was getting filled with ingenious industries, and rising to be what it still is, the busiest quarter of Germany. A country lowing with kine; the hum of the flax-spindle heard in its cottages in those old days—'much of the linen called Hollands is made in Jülich, and only bleached, stamped, and sold by the Dutch,' says Büsching. A country in our days which is shrouded at short intervals with the due canopy of coal-smoke, and loud with sounds of the anvil and the loom.

The lawyers took two hundred and six years to settle the question concerning this duchy, and the thing Johann Sigismund had claimed legally in 1609 was actually handed over to Johann Sigismund's descendant in the seventh generation. 'These litigated duchies are now the Prussian provinces, Jülich, Berg, Cleve, and the nucleus of Prussia's possessions in the Rhine country.'

X. George Wilhelm. Read pp. 325 to 327 (231, 333) on this Elector and German Protestantism, now fallen cold, and somewhat too little dangerous. But George Wilhelm is the only weak prince of all the twelve. For another example how the heart and life of a country depend upon its prince, not on its council, read this, of Gustavus Adolphus demanding the cession of Spandau and Küstrin:

Which cession Kurfürst George Wilhelm, though giving all his prayers to the good cause, could by no means grant. Gustav had to insist, with more and more emphasis, advancing at last with military menace upon Berlin itself. He was met by George Wilhelm and his Council, 'in the woods of Cöpenick,' short way to the east of that city; there George Wilhelm and his Council wandered about, sending messages, hopelessly consulting, saying among each other, 'Que faire? ils ont des canons.' For many hours so, round the inflexible Gustav, who was there like a fixed milestone, and to all questions and comers had only one answer.

On our special question of war and its consequences, read this of the Thirty years' one:

But, on the whole, the grand weapon in it, and, towards the latter times, the exclusive one, was hunger. The opposing armies tried to starve one another; at lowest, tried each not to starve. Each trying to eat the country, or, at any rate, to leave nothing eatable in it; what that will mean for the country we may consider. As the armies too frequently, and the Kaiser's armies habitually, lived without commissariat, often enough without pay, all horrors of war and of being a seat of war, that have been since heard of, are poor to those then practised, the detail of which is still horrible to read. Germany, in all eatable quarters of it, had to undergo the process; tortured, torn to pieces, wrecked, and brayed as in a mortar, under the iron mace of war. Brandenburg saw its towns seized and sacked, its country populations driven to despair by the one party and the other. Three times—first in the Wallenstein-Mecklenburg times, while fire and sword were the weapons, and again, twice over, in the ultimate stages of the struggle, when starvation had become the method—Brandenburg fell to be the principal theatre of conflict, where all forms of the dismal were at their height. In 1638, three years after that precious 'Peace of Prag,' * * * * the ravages of the starving Gallas and his Imperialists excelled all precedent, * * * * men ate human flesh, nay, human creatures ate their own children.' 'Que faire? ils ont des canons!'

'We have now arrived at the lowest nadir point' (says Carlyle) 'of the history of Brandenburg under the Hohenzollerns.' Is this then all that Heavy Peg and our nine Kurfürsts have done for us?

Carlyle does not mean that: but even he, greatest of historians since Tacitus, is not enough careful to mark for us the growth of national character, as distinct from the prosperity of dynasties.

A republican historian would think of this development only, and suppose it to be possible without any dynasties.

Which is indeed in a measure so; and the work now chiefly needed in moral philosophy, as well as history, is an analysis of the constant and prevalent, yet unthought of, influences, which, without any external help from kings, and in a silent and entirely necessary manner, form, in Sweden, in Bavaria, in the Tyrol, in the Scottish border, and on the French sea-coast, races of noble peasants; pacific, poetic, heroic, Christian-hearted in the deepest sense, who may indeed perish by sword or famine in any cruel thirty years' war, or ignoble thirty years' peace, and yet leave such strength to their children that the country, apparently ravaged into hopeless ruin, revives, under any prudent king, as the cultivated fields do under the spring rain. How the rock to which no seed can cling, and which no rain can soften, is subdued into the good ground which can bring forth its hundred-fold, we forget to watch, while we follow the footsteps of the sower, or mourn the catastrophes of storm. All this while, the Prussian earth,—the Prussian soul,—has been thus dealt upon by successive fate; and now, though laid, as it seems, utterly desolate, it can be revived by a few years of wisdom and of peace.

Vol. I., Book III. Chap. xviii.—The Great Elector, Friedrich Wilhelm. Eleventh of the dynasty: —

There hardly ever came to sovereign power a young man of twenty under more distressing, hopeless-looking circumstances. Political significance Brandenburg had none; a mere Protestant appendage, dragged about by a Papist Kaiser. His father's Prime Minister, as we have seen, was in the interest of his enemies; not Brandenburg's servant, but Austria's. The very commandants of his fortresses, Commandant of Spandau more especially, refused to obey

Friedrich Wilhelm on his accession; 'were bound to obey the Kaiser in the first place.'

For twenty years past Brandenburg had been scoured by hostile armies, which, especially the Kaiser's part of which, committed outrages new in human history. In a year or two hence, Brandenburg became again the theatre of business, Austrian Gallas advancing thither again (1644) with intent 'to shut up Torstenson and his Swedes in Jutland.' Gallas could by no means do what he intended; on the contrary, he had to run from Torstenson—what feet could do; was hunted, he and his Merode Brüder (beautiful inventors of the 'marauding' art), till they pretty much all died (crepirten) says Köhler. No great loss to society, the death of these artists, but we can fancy what their life, and especially what the process of their dying, may have cost poor Brandenburg again!

Friedrich Wilhelm's aim, in this as in other emergencies, was sun-clear to himself, but for most part dim to everybody else. He had to walk very warily, Sweden on one hand of him, suspicious Kaiser on the other; he had to wear semblances, to be ready with evasive words, and advance noiselessly by many circuits. More delicate operation could not be imagined. But advance he did; advance and arrive. With extraordinary talent, diligence, and felicity the young man wound himself out of this first fatal position, got those foreign armies pushed out of his country, and kept them out. His first concern had been to find some vestige of revenue, to put that upon a clear footing, and by loans or otherwise to scrape a little ready-money together. On the strength *of which a small body of soldiers could be collected about him, and drilled into real ability to fight and obey.* This as a basis: on this followed all manner of things, freedom from Swedish-Austrian invasions, as the first thing. He was himself, as appeared by-and-by, a fighter of the first quality, when it came to that; but never was willing to fight if he could help it. Preferred rather to shift, manœuvre, and negotiate, which he did in most vigilant, adroit, and masterly manner. But by degrees he had grown to have, and could maintain it, an army of 24,000 men, among the best troops then in being.

To wear semblances, to be ready with evasive words, how is this, Mr. Carlyle? thinks perhaps the rightly thoughtful reader.

Yes, such things have to be. There are lies and lies, and there are truths and truths. Ulysses cannot ride on the ram's back, like Phryxus; but must ride under his belly. Read also this, presently following:

Shortly after which, Friedrich Wilhelm, who had shone much in the battle of Warsaw, into which he was dragged against his will, changed sides. An inconsistent, treacherous man? Perhaps not, O reader! perhaps a man advancing 'in circuits,' the only way he has; spirally, face now to east, now to west, with his own reasonable private aim sun-clear to him all the while?

The battle of Warsaw, three days long, fought with Gustavus, the grandfather of Charles XII. against the Poles, virtually ends the Polish power:

Old Johann Casimir, not long after that peace of Oliva, getting tired of his unruly Polish chivalry and their ways, abdicated—retired to Paris and, 'lived much with Ninon de l'Enclos and her circle,' for the rest of his life. He used to complain of his Polish chivalry, that there was no solidity in them; nothing but outside glitter, with tumult and anarchic noise; fatal want of one essential talent, *the talent of obeying;* and has been heard to prophesy that a glorious Republic, persisting in such courses, would arrive at results which would surprise it.

Onward from this time, Friedrich Wilhelm figures in the world; public men watching his procedure; kings anxious to secure him—Dutch print-sellers sticking up his portraits for a hero-worshipping public. Fighting hero, had the public known it, was not his essential character, though he had to fight a great deal. He was essentially an industrial man; great in organizing, regulating, in constraining chaotic heaps to become cosmic for him. He drains bogs, settles colonies in the waste places of his dominions, cuts canals; unweariedly encourages trade and work. The Friedrich Wilhelm's Canal, which still carries tonnage from the Oder to the Spree, is a monument of his zeal in this way; creditable with the means he had. To the poor French Protestants in the Edict-of-Nantes affair, he was like an express benefit of Heaven; one helper appointed to whom the help itself was profitable. He munificently welcomed them to Brandenburg; showed really a noble piety and human pity, as well as judgment; nor did Brandenburg and he want their reward. Some 20,000 nimble French souls, evidently of the best French quality, found a home there; made 'waste sands about Berlin into potherb gardens;' and in spiritual Brandenburg, too, did something of horticulture which is still noticeable.

Now read carefully the description of the man, p. 352; (224–5); the story of the battle of Fehrbellin, 'the Marathon of Brandenburg,' p. 354 (225); and of the winter campaign of 1679, p. 356 (227), beginning with its week's marches at sixty miles a day; his wife, as always, being with him:

Louisa, honest and loving Dutch girl, aunt to our William of Orange, who trimmed up her own 'Orange-burg' (country-house), twenty miles north of Berlin, into a little jewel of the Dutch type, potherb gardens, training-schools for young girls, and the like, a favourite abode of hers when she was at liberty for recreation. But her life was busy and earnest; she was helpmate, not in name only, to an ever busy man. They were married young; a marriage of love withal. Young Friedrich Wilhelm's courtship; wedding in Holland; the honest, trustful walk and conversation of the two sovereign spouses, their journeyings together, their mutual hopes, fears, and manifold vicissitudes, till death, with stern beauty, shut it in; all is human, true, and wholesome in it, interesting to look upon, and rare among sovereign persons.

Louisa died in 1667, twenty-one years before her husband, who married again—(little to his contentment)—died in 1688; and Louisa's second son, Friedrich, ten years old at his mother's death, and now therefore thirty-one, succeeds, becoming afterwards Friedrich I. of Prussia.

And here we pause on two great questions. Prussia is assuredly at this point a happier and better country than it was, when inhabited by Wends. But is Friedrich I. a happier and better man than Henry the Fowler? Have all these kings thus improved

14

their country, but never themselves? Is this somewhat expensive and ambitious Herr, Friedrich I., buttoned in diamonds, indeed the best that Protestantism can produce, as against Fowlers, Bears, and Red Beards? Much more, Friedrich Wilhelm, orthodox on predestination; most of all, his less orthodox son;—have we, in these, the highest results which Dr. Martin Luther can produce, for the present, in the first circles of society? And if not, how is it that the country, having gained so much in intelligence and strength, lies more passively in their power than the baser country did under that of nobler men?

These, and collateral questions, I mean to work out as I can, with Carlyle's good help;—but must pause for this time; in doubt, as heretofore. Only of this one thing I doubt not, that the name of all great kings, set over Christian nations, must at last be, in fulfilment, the hereditary one of these German princes, 'Rich in Peace;' and that their coronation will be with Wild olive, not with gold.

LONDON: PRINTED BY
SPOTTISWOODE AND CO., NEW-STREET SQUARE
AND PARLIAMENT STREET